PRAISE FOR *COUNTRY QUEERS*

"'We are everywhere.' You've heard it said, and with *Country Queers* 1
makes it plain. This book is such a gift to rural queer folks. It renders us visible. Renders
our past and present experiences, questions, and struggles to navigate complicated
feelings about people and place visible. More broadly, *Country Queers* reminds us all
that even in the smallest places, in the 'reddest' states, there have always been queer
people fighting for our collective liberation. They demand our solidarity. They, and
this book, demand our close attention because they have so much to teach us."
—NEEMA AVASHIA, author of *Another Appalachia: Coming
Up Queer and Indian in a Mountain Place*

"With the art of a storyteller Rae Garringer expands our understanding of queer
lives and shows that our home places are everywhere we want them to be."
—BARBARA SMITH, author of *The Truth That Never Hurts:
Writings on Race, Gender, and Freedom*

"Rae Garringer's work speaks directly to the all-too-common experience of
loving a place that doesn't always love you back. *Country Queers* is a map of
queer resilience and placemaking. It serves as an artifact for the next generations
of queer misfits making sense of the complex spaces we call home."
—ASHBY COMBAHEE, cofounder of Georgia Dusk: a southern liberation oral history
project, and librarian and archivist at Highlander Research and Education Center

"For over eleven years, writer and oral historian Rae Garringer has been thoughtfully
listening to and documenting the experiences of queer people living in rural America,
and now they have gathered these remarkable stories to share with readers.
What a gift! *Country Queers* is a tender, fierce, and inspiring love letter to a
population that is too often made invisible. Garringer serves as a generous
and attentive guide, shining a light on stories of queer joy, courage, and fierce
resistance. An important and necessary book, and a beautiful triumph."
—CARTER SICKELS, author of *The Prettiest Star*

"This is indeed the love letter of the subtitle: to the country, to queer friends and neighbors, to the small pieces of life. Slow down and flip through this uplifting, hand-threaded quilt of lives."
—KIRKUS REVIEWS

"Rae Garringer and their interview companions pay homage to the back roads, hollers, hills, hell-raising, heartbreak, love affairs, and joys of small town and country queer life. Across geography, generations, and gender, *Country Queers* gives voice to a lineage of queer and trans people claiming our seat at the table."
—HERMELINDA CORTÉS, executive director of ReFrame

"On page after page, readers meet charismatic country queers whose words are joined with Garringer's travelogue—a road trip story propelled by gnawing queer love for country and a wish to (peripatetically) 'return home.' This is queer history at its best, making a play on oral history's superpower to complicate a narrative that has long gone undiscerned, undetected, and oversimplified. Garringer reminds us that country queers 'have always made a way out of no way' and tells us how."
—SUZANNE SNIDER, founder/director of Oral History Summer School

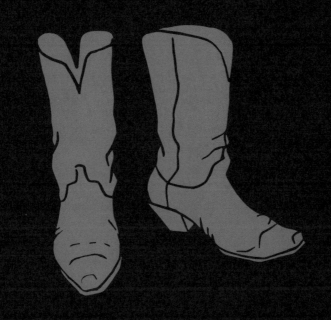

COUNTRY

A LOVE

HAYMARKET BOOKS
CHICAGO, IL

QUEERS
LETTER

RAE
GARRINGER

This book has been made possible through a grant from
the West Virginia Humanities Council, a state affiliate of the
National Endowment for the Humanities.

ISBN: 979-8-88890-248-6
Distributed to the trade in the US through Consortium Book Sales and Distribution (www.cbsd.com)
and internationally through Ingram Publisher Services International (www.ingramcontent.com).

This book was published with the generous support of Lannan Foundation,
Wallace Action Fund, and Marguerite Casey Foundation.
Special discounts are available for bulk purchases by organizations and institutions.
Please email info@haymarketbooks.org for more information.

All photographs by Rae Garringer unless noted otherwise.
Page iii: cowboy boots (appearing here and throughout) drawn by Rae Garringer
Page 1: "Danger God Loves Country Queers" hoop embroidery made by Elizabeth Sanders
Page 4: "Country Queers Can Survive & Thrive" sticker drawn by Rae Garringer
Page 7: "Queer Scout" badge made by Mary Tremonte at Just Seeds
Page 15: unicorn bolo tie made by Elliot M. Evans at Small Time Shirts
Page 16: "Country" and "Queer" sequin hearts made by Grier L.
Page 150: possum bolo tie made by Raina Rue at Juniper Moon Folk Arts
Cover and interior design by Eric Kerl.
Printed in Canada by union labor.
Library of Congress Cataloging-in-Publication data is available.

1 3 5 7 9 10 8 6 4 2

For country queers past who cleared a path,
and for all those present and future who will continue to travel it

CONTENTS

Foreword *by Suzanne Pharr* 1
Preface 3
Editorial Note 15

THE FIRST YEAR: 2013   17
Elandria Williams *Knoxville, Tennessee* 23
Sam Gleaves *Wytheville, Virginia* 29
"Frances" *Western Massachusetts* 33

THE ROAD TRIP: 2014   39
Mason Michael *Southern Mississippi* 43
Sandra Vera *Lake Jackson, Texas* 51
David Rodriguez *Bastrop, Texas* 55
Allie Gartman *Big Spring, Texas* 61
Crisosto Apache *Denver, Colorado* 67
Wil Garten and Loring Wagner *Edmond, Oklahoma* 75
Crystal Middlestadt *Ribera, New Mexico* 85
Twig Delujé *Pecos, New Mexico* 89
Cameron McCoy *Avondale, Colorado* 93

THE OVERWHELM: 2015–2019   97
Sharon P. Holland *Chapel Hill, North Carolina* 101
Robyn Thirkill *Prospect, Virginia* 107
Tessa Eskander *Cookeville, Tennessee* 113
Silas House *Berea, Kentucky* 117
Dorothy Allison *Guerneville, California* 121

THE PANDEMIC ERA: 2020–2023   127

Penelope Logue *Westcliffe, Colorado* 133
Suzanne Pharr *Little Rock, Arkansas* 139
Kijana West *Cumberland, Maryland* 145
Ty Walker *Cumberland, Maryland* 151
Kasha Snyder-McDonald *Charleston, West Virginia* 157

Postscript: "A Wholeness to Our Lives":
  A Conversation between hermelinda cortés and Rae Garringer 167
Acknowledgments 171

FOREWORD

This book is a narrative of pain, heartbreak, courage, and joy. It shows us that queers raised in rural and small-town places do not occupy the same *country* as urban queers. Reading each person's narrative, I can't help wondering what it would have meant had they known the lived experiences of other people out there struggling, celebrating, surviving, floundering, and flourishing.

It can be said that all queers long for a community that understands and accepts them. The history of violence against queer people has forced us to create—and beautifully, I should say—communities that hold us with the acknowledgement that we exist and that we are of worth. For country queers, finding or building this community is a Herculean task. In rural areas, for everyone community is everything, and schools and churches are the primary places of connection. With few resources, people reach out to each other.

In *Country Queers: A Love Letter*, we see the narrow edge that rural queers live on. To find and build queer community, they have to come out, and if they do come out, they risk losing the only community they have, the one that raised them.

I grew up on a farm in Hog Mountain, Georgia, in the 1940s. As I grappled with my own queerness, I struggled with what I might lose if I chose visibility and freedom: the love of my very large farm family, my acceptance in the church I grew up in and among the families and friends within it, my sense of belonging in a physical place I loved. Queers on this journey ask ourselves, "If we lose these, what else is left?" And the answer we discover is "the freedom to be."

Through combining oral history interviews with the narrative of their own life as a country queer, Rae brings alive stories of survival and loss, as well as the joys of freedom. We hear stories of violence, HIV/ AIDS, religious condemnation, rejection by friends and family, the double-edged sword of racism and homophobia—and we learn of the joy of meeting another queer or trans person in a town where we thought there was no one, of building a lesbian land project, of creating secret communities where we can meet others, of organizing Pride events where we can all move toward visibility and the joy of belonging.

All of these stories are held together by the thread of Rae's own love of the country and their desire for themself and others to be free. It is a beautifully detailed account of their journey to create the *Country Queers* podcast, intertwined with intimate details of their own discovery and growth. Rae's honesty, attention to detail, love of the people they meet, courage, and determination makes this book inspirational in the best sense of the word—let it be encouragement for all of us to work to create inclusive communities of care for all.

SUZANNE PHARR

Wahzhazhe (Osage), O-gah-pah (Quapaw), and Očhéthi Šakówiŋ (Oglala Sioux) lands
Little Rock, Arkansas
April 2024

Suzanne Pharr is a southern queer feminist who organizes on the front lines of gender, race, and economics. Her work has been with multiracial, multiissue organizations: founder of the Women's Project in Arkansas, cofounder of Southerners on New Ground, director of the Highlander Center, and founding member of the Southern Movement Assembly. Pharr is the author of *Transformation: Toward a People's Democracy*, *In the Time of the Right: Reflections on Liberation*, and *Homophobia: A Weapon of Sexism*. For more, visit www.suzannepharr.com.

PREFACE

Early in 2011, I was sitting in midafternoon bumper-to-bumper traffic in Austin, Texas, behind the wheel of my then girlfriend's pink-and-purple-striped, 1980s Chevy van. It had been her family's van when she was a kid; later it had become her all-girl country band's tour mobile. It was big enough for us to camp in, which we did anytime I could convince her to get out of the city with me. Even though we were months away from summer, it was already hot in Texas, and I had the windows rolled down because the van had no air-conditioning. I'd been living in Austin for three years, and it had been nine years since I'd left the sheep farm where I was raised, high up in the Allegheny Mountains of southeastern West Virginia. Since leaving home, I hadn't stopped missing the mountains. I was constantly aware of their absence, as if their silhouettes were tattooed across the inside of my eyelids so that I saw them every time I closed my eyes.

I had fun in Austin. I rode my bike all over town and ate so many tacos. I swam in January and fell in love with the prickly charm of cactus and agave. I became a regular at a gay country bar—first the Rainbow Cattle Company, then the newly opened Rusty Spurs—the first places I ever saw queerness and country-ness embrace one another. Through those years of aching homesickness, that bar became my church, and the other regulars my chosen family. They took me to the gay rodeo (and the straight rodeo, too). They taught me to two-step, and that partner dancing doesn't have to reinforce heteronormative gender roles—that you can be a switch on the dance floor, too. On holidays, when my income from waiting tables didn't come close to covering the cost of a plane ticket home, they invited me over for dinner.

On that day in early 2011, traffic was at a standstill. Since the radio in the van didn't work either, I started singing my favorite Hazel Dickens song, "West Virginia, My Home."

It's been years now since I left there
and this city life's about got the best of me

3

The traffic inched forward, and I kept singing, until suddenly I was crying.

Home, home, home
Oh, I can see it so clear in my mind
Home, home, home
I can almost smell the honeysuckle vine

That April, I moved back home to West Virginia and rented my childhood neighbor's small white farmhouse for two hundred dollars a month, on land that bordered my stepdad's sheep farm, where I was raised. After returning home, I felt a sense of completeness, of being able to breathe deeper than I had in years. I felt an unfamiliar sureness about my place in the world and a calm rootedness I had never experienced before in my life. I felt like I could finally rest inside the strong embrace of these mountains, with the soothing sounds of sheep floating gently in through open windows.

Back in high school, I rode the bus for four hours a day—useless hours of kids snorting pills, bloodying each other's noses with their fists, fooling around, listening to Walkmans, spitting tobacco juice into empty Dr. Pepper bottles. One morning on the bus in 2001, my friend Shawn called me a lesbian after I cut my waist-length hair short and close to my head during spring break of my sophomore year. I whine-argued back "I am not!" Years later, after Shawn fatally overdosed on heroin while I was in graduate school in North Carolina, I realized in my grieving that while "lesbian" isn't a word I claim for myself, he had been the first person to name my queerness out loud.

I now know that I had met four lesbians and two gay men in West Virginia before I left for college. None of them were explicitly out, but everyone talked. "There's only one bed in the house," or "Neither of them have ever been married." The trans woman up the road was ridiculed by adults all around me when she transitioned. In hindsight, I can see their queerness, their gender expansiveness. Now, they shimmer and glow in the cherished haze of my memory. But at the time, I didn't recognize myself in any of them.

The most memorable West Virginia lesbian from this era was the butch Department of Natural Resources officer who came to my eighth-grade Career Day. I still remember her short hair, military-green uniform, and bourbon-colored boots. I had never heard the word "lesbian" before my friends whispered it as she walked by us in the hall, but middle schoolers are hardwired to pick up on subtle social cues. It's a strategy of survival. So I said, "Ewww!" before asking what that word meant. I acted bored during her presentation, but I had made damn sure to be there.

Later that same year, I spent the night at my friend Sandy's house. I remember her mom—who sported that classic feathery 1980s white-dyke-mullet, wore pants pulled up high and tightly belted over a tucked-in button-up, and always had a can of beer glued to one hand. They rented a two-story house in the county seat. It had faux-wood paneling on the walls and carpet that smelled of cigarette smoke. I remember Sandy's mom scooping her up onto her shoulder with one arm, then tossing her down onto the couch, all while never setting down her beer. Upstairs that afternoon, Sandy curled my hair and did my makeup, like a real girl. That night, I got drunk for the first time, on Jägermeister, with her and a bunch of high school boys. Later, in the empty streets downtown, the boys fought, one wielding a baseball bat. I remember my fear, dizzy, out in the street with older boys whose handsy interest was both a compliment to my fragile middle-school ego and a queasy terror. But mostly, I remember thinking about the way

my friend's mom had moved earlier that evening: shoulders broad and tight, veined hands strong, jaw hard, with a mixture of awe and discomfort spinning inside of me.

Still, I didn't recognize my own queerness, and I waded through the hell of high school avoiding dating altogether. On the bus one morning a boy said, "We should put all the faggots on an island and drop a bomb on them." Everyone laughed but me. I remember wanting to get as far away from West Virginia as I could. I wanted to leave more than I'd ever wanted anything. And I did, because unlike many of my peers, I had the privilege of being able to do so.

I quickly learned that I was queer during my first semester at college in western Massachusetts in 2003. I had been raised by hippies with no TV, and we got slow, dial-up internet late in my teenage years. I now know there were queer kids finding each other in online chat rooms and watching *Will and Grace* and *Ellen* on TV, but I hadn't had access to any of that at the time. Before going to college, I'd never seen androgyny or gender queerness among people my age. I didn't know it was a possibility for me— to embody or to desire—until I left these mountains for a place where all my new peers came from coastal cities and, for the most part, from immense wealth. I didn't realize how much disdain so much of this country has for the rural South until those four years in the Northeast. I didn't even know for sure I was *from* the South until I left. I also didn't know, until I moved back home to West Virginia years later, that there were indeed queer folks my age in these mountains. And that being queer and country at the same time was not only possible but would turn out to be one of the most healing experiences of my life.

Back home in 2011, after years in Massachusetts and Texas, I started to recognize other queer people when I drove into town. At the Walmart, we'd give each other the subtlest of nods, the kind no one else would notice. Or we'd completely ignore each other, a self-protective strategy that no one ever explicitly taught me but that all country queers must learn. I'd see queers at the state fair. They'd linger a little longer at the pen where I helped my goat mentor get her Alpine dairy goats ready for competition. I'd blush, feeling their eyes on me, and look away, unsure how to *do* queerness here. Do we talk? Do we not? Do we stick together or scatter?

Despite my new awareness of our presence here and the great joy and relief I found in moving home, I started to feel extremely isolated from queer and political community. I realized that while my queer friends in cities across the country would always be important in my life, I needed to find people who understood how to navigate the tension of loving a place unconditionally, even while some community members tell you, "You don't belong here." I wanted to meet people who had insights about how to date, build community, and create expansive queer

families in *rural* places. I needed to connect with people who understood that the quietness around queerness in many small southern towns doesn't only feel oppressive but also sometimes feels like a compromise, a way for community members to navigate difference in the most respectful way for all involved—something rural people are often very skilled at, and others could learn from. And I was curious about the ways in which rural LGBTQIA2S+ experiences are similar and different across intersecting layers of identities, including those of race, class, age, and ability.

I also began to recognize my growing frustration about how the historical presence and contemporary existence of rural queer and trans people had been so thoroughly erased from national queer media and organizing landscapes that I had truly believed, before moving home, that there weren't any queer people here. At the same time, I grew agitated that our very own home communities, all across this country, had lied to us by omission about the fact that we have always been here. Queers, in all our forms, have always existed, all across this continent, since before it was colonized.

There is a whole lot more rural queer visibility today than there was in 2013. Back then, an online search for "rural queer" or "small-town gay" came up almost empty. The only widely known rural queer stories were those of the brutal murder of Matthew Shepard and the horrifying rape and murder of Brandon Teena, made famous by the 1999 film *Boys Don't Cry*. The fictional film *Brokeback Mountain*, was released in 2005, bringing a rural gay love story to the big screen—though, again, it centers gay white cisgender men, one of whom is murdered. I'm 1,000 percent here for butch4butch gay cowboy stories, but until very recently, in literally *every* film featuring rural queer characters, one of them is killed in the end. I now know

that there were already complex rural queer stories buried deep within gorgeous novels by so many southern writers, including Randall Kenan, Fenton Johnson, and Dorothy Allison. But none of these novels made their way to a queer kid in Pocahontas County, West Virginia, circa 1998.

Country Queers emerged out of a desire to seek out stories of rural queerness that move beyond tales of violence and despair, as well as out of my personal need for connection born of isolation. In the more than ten years since the first interview was recorded, Country Queers has evolved into a community-based multimedia oral history project. The project has grown from its humble beginnings as a handful of writings and transcripts on a blog to a collection of over ninety oral histories, a gallery exhibit, and a podcast. And now, the original dream of a book has come true. But the journey to this point has been long and meandering.

When I started Country Queers, I had no formal training in oral history or audio recording. I had three part-time jobs in three counties and barely enough income to make ends meet. But I had an abundance of curiosity and stubborn determination. The first interviews I recorded in the summer of 2013 were with friends I had met through the Stay Together Appalachian Youth Project—a network of young people who are committed to supporting one another in making Appalachia a place where they can and want to stay. STAY was the space where I found the queer and political community I'd been missing. It was the network that provided me with the support and encouragement I needed to set out on this ambitious quest to document rural and small-town LGBTQIA2S+ stories. Those first interviews were recorded at STAY's annual Summer Institute, which took place at the Highlander Research and Education Center—a historic popular education center in the mountains of east Tennessee. On paisley-patterned couches in dorm rooms, on wooden benches on the porch of the workshop center, I stiffly and awkwardly asked those first questions. I can still picture each of those early interviews, and I remember being more nervous than the people I was interviewing seemed to be.

All these years and interviews later, I am still amazed that it worked at all. I have learned so much from trying things, making mistakes, and trying again. I have learned from countless conversations with trusted friends and mentors over the years, and also from conversations with journalists and academics whose approaches to this work I have strong reservations about. I have learned from books, lectures, articles, and films. But the most important lessons in how to do this work—ethically, humbly, and responsibly—have come from the people who have agreed to sit down and share some of their stories with me. To this day, every time I leave an interview, I am floored by the trust, generosity, and vulnerability that narrators offer to me. It feels like a gift each and every time—one that deserves fierce protection and respect. There is something deeply sacred to me about these intimate rural queer exchanges.

People often ask me to summarize common themes of rural queer experiences that I've gleaned through this work. I hate that question, not because it's a bad one but because "rural" and "country" are words that hold multitudes, full of complicated and often contradictory associations. I recently learned that the US Census Bureau defines "rural" as "all population, housing, and territory not included within an urban area"—a category so amorphous it makes me laugh.

LGBTQIA2S+ people are nothing if not experts at arguing over and pushing for the evolution of language, for new ways to name and describe ourselves. Part of what I love about the word "queer" is that it isn't a narrowing or restrictive container. It's a word big enough to hold so many different experiences that when I claim it for myself, I don't feel tightly boxed in by it. I love how similarly expansive "country" is, so much more than just a geographic descriptor. Strangely, I love, too, how loaded it is for so many of us. "Country" is a word weighed down by centuries of history around colonization, genocide, forced removal, enslavement, violence, agriculture, mineral rights, natural resource extraction, class, faith, music, migration, climate disaster, joy, resilience, community care, pride, and so much more. I love how complicated it is, how messy even at times. I love that it can't be neatly tied up with a bow.

Of course, I have opinions based on my own experiences about what feels like a small town versus a city, and if you catch me after a whiskey or two, you might hear me talk some shit. But I know well that there are countless rural and small-town LGBTQIA2S+ experiences very different from my own. I decided early on in this project that I had no interest in policing a concept or definition of what does or doesn't "count" as country, small town, or rural based on population numbers alone. Major cities are out—though some people once tried to convince me that Atlanta is "country." Across all these interviews with all these people in all these places, only a few things seem universal: most country queers *detest* sitting in traffic and do not understand why city people put up with it; the isolation can be real intense at times; and, for many of us, dating is *rough* out here.

My hope is that the Country Queers project has provided an antidote to the feelings of isolation so common among rural queer people, and that it has added nuance to the long-standing national narrative that positions metropolitan spaces as safe for LGBTQIA2S+ people and rural spaces as unsafe. This oversimplification flattens the deep complexity and multidimensionality of all our communities.

In the past decade, representations of rural and small-town LGBTQIA2S+ folks have grown, and Instagram in particular has seen a boom in our visibility. There are popular TV shows like *Schitt's Creek* and *We're Here* that explore rural queer experiences. There are occasional national magazine or news articles about the gay rodeo circuit or queer farmers. There has also been an increase in books digging into queer rurality over the past decade, and new queer country musicians seem to emerge onto the scene each year. But as I watch this growth in visibility from this mountainside, I can't help but notice that most of this content is still being produced by people who are not personally living, *day in and day out*, the unique joys and challenges of rural queer life. There are real systemic reasons for this discrepancy. The connections and networks needed to break into publishing, filmmaking, podcasting, or journalism often don't exist in places like my home—not to mention the ongoing barriers many rural people face in trying to access reliable high-speed internet. Funding is incredibly hard to access for queer work here, particularly queer work with a radical or leftist politic. And rural people in general are often encouraged if not pressured to leave our homes for greater opportunities elsewhere.

When this project was born, I lived in a house with no cell service, no internet, and an old landline phone. Snakes came in through holes in the walls, and I commuted multiple hours a day to work in rural public schools where I couldn't be out. There have been unique challenges to running this project in and from rural Appalachia. But I also believe the project has benefited greatly from the fact that I have pecked away at it—week after week, month after month, year after year—as an isolated, chronically ill, visibly queer, and gender-weird person living in the conservative rural South, often with terrible (or no) internet access and

woefully subpar medical care. This work is not theoretical to me. It isn't a passion project born out of curiosity alone. It has been a personal strategy of survival.

I believe deeply in the power of marginalized communities reclaiming narratives about our people and places. Queer and trans people and rural folks have long been documented and studied by parachute journalists and academic "experts" with no lived experience of our identities or communities. Growing up in central Appalachia—a region with a long and complicated relationship to national media representation—I picked up quickly on the realities that storytelling work can often be damaging and extractive.

This project seeks to resist the long-standing patterns of extractive, unethical storytelling that are rampant in journalistic, academic, and documentary fields. That doesn't mean I have done this work perfectly. I don't believe perfection is possible, and these fields are riven with power dynamics. In the beginning of this project, I was not thinking nearly enough about colonization, forced removal, genocide, and enslavement in relation to rural spaces and land. I now recognize the inherent tensions present within this project—which aims to affirm and encourage a sense of belonging for

country queers in places where we've long been told we don't belong—because the majority of narrators in this collection, including myself, are descendants of colonizers occupying stolen Indigenous land. What does it mean for white country queers to find a sense of belonging through our relationships to land when that comes at the expense of Indigenous people's displacement from their own lands and erasure from our local and regional histories? What does it mean for descendants of enslaved folks to be in relationship to land their ancestors were forced to work, in an ongoing context of rampant Black land theft? What is the responsibility of white country queers in movements around reparations and returning stolen land to Indigenous stewardship? This project hasn't answered these questions definitively. But, in talking about the power dynamics and imperfections underlying documentary work, it is important to acknowledge that these tensions exist. This book will not resolve them, but I hope that it can hold some of this profound complexity within its pages.

My desire for this book and this project is to offer a necessary intervention into conversations about rural spaces at a national level that rarely center the voices and lived experience of rural people. This project positions rural queer and trans narrators as the experts of their own lives, communities, and histories. The Country Queers project has always been, first and foremost, an offering to other isolated rural and small-town LGBTQIA2S+ people. I want every rural queer person reading this book, after a hard day of feeling unseen or unsupported, to know that there are many of us out here riding these waves of grief and joy, each of us wondering, at times, if we are the only ones still committed to building this kind of life in this kind of place, in these deeply polarized times.

Over the past decade, I've recorded interviews with country queers in twenty-

one states, from Texas to Massachusetts, from Colorado to Kentucky. The youngest was nineteen, and the eldest was eighty-one. Among them are farmers, small-town politicians, teachers, gay-rodeo competitors, Walmart clerks, artists, organizers, drag performers, professors, dining hall managers, hotel employees, carpenters, and writers.

One of the gifts working on this book has offered me has been the chance, for the first time, to look back at this collection of interviews as a whole. While there has been great beauty in that process, it has also underscored what I fretted over for years: there is a dearth of stories from Indigenous narrators, from migrants, and from femmes, among other communities. Word of mouth was my primary tool for finding narrators in

the early years, when the majority of these interviews were recorded, and my network in rural spaces at that time was predominantly white. Another factor in those gaps was the structural, historical reality of out-migration, secrecy, silence, and the losses of the AIDS epidemic. It is also worth noting that two of the narrators I'd hoped to include in this book, both women of color, did not feel safe with the increased visibility that this would bring. These gaps notwithstanding, this book tells some of the story of the evolution of this project and of my approach to this work.

In the pages ahead, you'll meet some of the delightful country queers I've had the honor of interviewing. You'll read edited excerpts from their interviews and some reflections and gratitude from me about our conversations. You'll see some of their faces and the places they call home through photographs I made during my travels. You'll also see some of the ephemera I've gathered along the way. There will be bolo ties, handsewn gifts I've received, and shots of blurry landscapes caught out the window of a moving car. The book moves chronologically through the project's history, and the narrators are mostly presented in the order they were interviewed. At the book's conclusion, you'll find a conversation between me and hermelinda cortés—an

advisor to the project, a brilliant organizer, and a country queer too—reflecting on what we think Country Queers has accomplished over the years.

Even after a decade of trying to prove, for myself and for others, that we *do* exist everywhere, there are times still when I feel like my sense of isolation from queer and trans community is my fault. I know that this is a systemic failing, but it's easy to believe that if I would only make different choices—like move to Durham or Asheville or Middle Tennessee—then I wouldn't be so isolated. There are days when everything feels like an uphill battle—from the broken lawnmower and escape-artist goats to a coal train derailment in the river and a state legislature hell-bent on blocking trans people's access to health care. As I write this, legislative and physical attacks on trans and queer people are sweeping the nation, and it feels like conservatives are trying to legislate us out of existence while right-wing militants are killing us in our bars and in the streets. It becomes clearer to me every day that small towns and conservative cities across the South, Midwest, and West are the new front lines in the battle for queer and trans liberation. And yet our organizing efforts persist, scrappily, despite drastically less access to funding, support, and infrastructure than many of those under way in major cities. It is daunting, infuriating, and terrifying to watch this unfold in real time.

Still, I believe in rural queer people. We have always made a way out of no way. We have always found one another hiding in plain sight. We have always resisted and lovingly pushed our communities forward in ways that may seem too quiet and too slow to people used to a city pace or pitch, but that *work* in our communities. We have always been here, and we always will be. We will continue to claim our joy, in public and in private. We will continue to protect and care for each other. And no amount of violent legislation or armed attacks on our people or places will ever succeed in erasing us from these hills and hollers, these deserts and plains, these mountains, salt marshes, beaches, and forests where we make our homes together, apart, beautifully, cozily, radically claiming our queerness and our country-ness at the same time.

RAE GARRINGER
S'atsoyaha (Yuchi) and Šaawanwaki
(Shawnee) lands
Southeastern West Virginia
March 2024

EDITORIAL NOTE

At the beginning of each oral history excerpt included in the pages ahead, we have named, to the best of our knowledge, the Indigenous stewards of the lands on which the narrators live. In a project focused on affirming the belonging of country queers, many of whom are descendants of settlers, on stolen land, it is imperative to situate individual rural queer narratives in a broader political and historical context, to unsettle the norms of how we talk about rural places and the nation-state currently known as the United States by recentering the Indigenous peoples whose lands we are on, and to foster conversations around what it means to be a good relative to those lands. We understand that this is a complicated, active, and ongoing conversation.

This decision did not emerge from the majority of narrator interviews themselves, but it is vital, particularly within a project dedicated to adding complexity, nuance, and depth to narratives about rural and country spaces.

Native place names were gathered from the incredible resource that is Native Land Digital (https://native-land.ca), an Indigenous-led nonprofit organization. Their website, which undergoes frequent updates, is comprehensive but by no means definitional; this information has been supplemented by preferred names as listed on tribal websites and other sources where possible. In many places, we have used multiple names for the same nation. We have also consulted with Indigenous linguists.

We understand that language is ever evolving and at times contested, and, in the years ahead, as we move toward reparations and returning stolen land to Indigenous stewardship, the conversation will likely be a different one. It is in this knowledge and spirit that we offer this note.

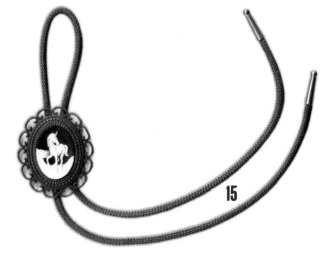

QUEER

COUNTRY

Country Queers
Thinking Book

...ill: at Ida & Sh...

Ma...
lan...

She-wolf —
(directory o...

...ike — ...is happening... co...
Lewis De...
Queers

many episodes?
... many a month?

...on-only episodes

full intervie...
...ot much... (not exc...
ep...

Co-host
vs
the host +
have reflections fro...
other ...
a...
...

producer — what d...
is host/dj — radio writer d no...
abt plotting out of...
producer
...mona will work on the str...
...p new interviews, d tape cutting
rights to music   editor
                          team

...y lesbian activists
   any sort ever
...anta Lesbian Fo...
closed

...y Eyes — The Culture of Q...
— J. Morris   © 1999
...nse to those who mock the idea
...not in Mississippi

THE FIRST YEAR

2013

In 2012, the beginnings of the idea for the Country Queers project were percolating, bouncing around in my mind during my free time—of which I had a lot. I was working three jobs across two large rural counties. I taught evening GED classes six hours a week in the county where I'd gone to high school. I taught as a substitute, both in adult basic education programs and public schools in the next county over, including at the elementary school I had attended as a child. The same principal was still there twenty-some years later. On my first day of substitute teaching he asked, "Didn't you used to have longer hair?" and then said, "I thought you'd be taller."

I also worked as a "standardized patient" at the School of Osteopathic Medicine in a nearby town, which may be one of the strangest jobs I've ever had. I'd pretend to be a patient with various health conditions memorized from a script, while medical students practiced diagnosing symptoms and their bedside manner. I quit after they told me my next assignment would be to act the part of a screaming, moaning pregnant person in labor pushing out a fake baby from a prosthetic belly.

I vividly remember sitting on the bed in a hospital gown during one of the long stretches between medical student visits, bored and kicking my feet, thinking: *What if I could take a road trip to interview other rural queer people?* I remember thinking there'd be no way I could afford that, and then wondering if I could fundraise to make it happen. I quickly thought, *There's no way in hell that will work.* But a year later, it did.

The idea started to solidify, greatly influenced by two events I attended. In May 2013, I drove to Knoxville, Tennessee, for a Stay Together Appalachian Youth (STAY)

Small Town Cross Roads
A Report by Southerners On New Ground

Project Fabulachian queer youth gathering. Then in June, I traveled back down to East Tennessee for Gaycation, organized by Southerners on New Ground (SONG), a nonprofit that serves as a political home for LGBTQ+ southerners fighting for racial and economic justice. At that first annual gathering, in an intergenerational, multiracial circle of thirty-some people, hermelinda cortés and Suzanne Pharr—both brilliant, southern country queers and organizers—led us in a conversation about our rural queer experiences across the South. I still remember hermelinda opening the space by asking us to describe what the places we called home smelled like in our memories. *Fresh cut hay. Rich earth. Grandmothers' cooking. Barn lofts. Clean country air.*

I came home all fired up and emailed one of my best friends, Ada Smith:

hey ada,

i've wanted to start this project interviewing country queers for a long time, put them on a blog, and maybe a book later? who knows. but i tend to drag my feet b/c i get scared to ask people if i can interview them.

i feel like i just need to start, because i am my own worst enemy sometimes, in terms of lacking the confidence to do shit.

i have two questions for you:

1. i wonder what you would want to know about other country queers lives/processes/passions/etc. i have some questions but want to get more feedback from others in the future on what folks would want to know…

2. i've been wanting to buy a voice recorder for years. finally am gonna do it. what was the recorder you suggested?

alright, see you soon,
–rae

She wrote back:

hey rae!

this sounds so huge and great and fun and SONG has talked about this and just go, go, go!

1. i'd want to know about having kids in small towns, about finding love, about hidden stories of the queers before them, how they negotiate with city queers and all the pressure to be in a city.

The rest of her email was equally encouraging, and it makes me smile now because neither of us had a clue as to the magnitude the project would take on in my life or how many future conversations we'd have about it. I recorded the first interview on July 2, 2013. I remember being so nervous to ask each question, worried I was just being nosy, certain I wasn't using the borrowed audio recorder correctly. I also remember feeling *elated* at the end. There was a kind of buzzy-ness to the air around that first interview, and I spent the next month thinking about it.

In early August, the STAY Project gathered for their annual Summer Institute at the Highlander Center. I recorded five interviews that weekend with fellow queer Appalachian young folks. Then in September, when I traveled up to the Northeast for a college bestie's wedding, I recorded two more interviews along the way. I barely knew how to use the recorder, and I was constantly worried I would accidently delete the files or forget to press record all together. I never wore headphones, and the audio quality of those first recordings is *terrible.*

That fall, during evenings at home, I sat next to the fire transcribing those long interviews by hand.* I didn't have internet or a cell phone. I'd never had my own social media accounts (and was adamantly opposed to them), so a friend started a Facebook page for the project using her account. On weekends, I'd go to the library in town and sit with my back to a wall, paranoid that if I sat by a walkway people would look over my shoulder and see "QUEER! QUEER! QUEER!" all over the screen as I uploaded the transcripts to my blog. I didn't know where this new obsession was headed, but I couldn't stop thinking about the handful of interviews gathered so far, and I couldn't wait to record more.

---

* Transcripts in this book were created by the author, some with support from online software, except in cases where volunteer transcriptionists are named. Photographs were taken by the author unless otherwise credited.

Pickett
St Park

Lincoln
Mem. Univ.

36

46

Cove
Lake 52

51

63

FOREST

Forest

Tennessee
Vil,

Gold
City

NANTAHALA

Lee Coll.

30

Cleveland

21

44

Hiwassee
Overflow Dam
307 Ft. High

NATIONAL FOREST

59

23

Elandria at the Highlander Center. Photo courtesy of E. Williams

ELANDRIA WILLIAMS they/them, 34 years old

Anitsalagi (Cherokee), S'atsoyaha (Yuchi), and Miccosukee lands
Knoxville, Tennessee
August 11, 2013

I first met Elandria, also known as E., in 2012 through the STAY Project. Over the next several years, I was blessed to get to learn from them, and to laugh and dance with them. Elandria was the kind of organizer whose brain and words moved so fast that the rest of us had to work hard to keep up. Without them, STAY wouldn't exist, and without that early STAY crew, Country Queers wouldn't exist.

I interviewed E. at the 2013 STAY Summer Institute, which took place at the Highlander Center, where they worked at the time. We spoke in the office building—which later, in 2019, would be burned down by white supremacists. On that hot August day, E. sat at the conference table, stapling together packets of paper for a workshop they were preparing to lead. We laughed a lot.

ELANDRIA: I live at the nexus of Appalachia and the South, in a city that thinks of itself as a town. Knoxville is the largest city in Appalachia, but one thing that's different about it from every other place I've been to is that nobody only hangs out with one type of people. It's not small enough where you feel like you have to close in and only hang with a certain type of people, and it's also not big enough where—especially if you're from here—you can just let go of all the people that you grew up with. You're almost forced to have friends that are cross race. You're forced to have friends that are everything. So my friend group is all races of people, but also all sexualities. Which is different than a lot of places where people only have lesbian friends or they only have gay boy friends or they only have trans friends. But I'm like, "Nope, I have friends that are all those categories, and all different races of those categories, and we all hang out together." It's beautiful, and it's one of the things I appreciate the most about Knoxville.

I was born here. The county where I grew up is mostly white, but I went to a pretty diverse school. I went to high school in Powell, *not* in a diverse school. As a young Black person, Powell *sucked*, in many ways, and I spent most of my time there doing organizing work trying to get rid of Confederate flags, trying to stop race fights, and all that. But they were good people. Because Powell was so intense, the people that I met there that I'm friends with, I'm *really* good friends with now.

I love basketball. It was actually all I really liked for a long time. My dad was a little freaked out about me playing on the basketball team because the coach was lesbian and he was like, "Oh my God, no!" So it was a fight to play sports, even though he wanted me to play, because he was like, "I already have a daughter who doesn't want to be a girl." So literally: I was not a girl in my life until I had a period and I thought I was internally bleeding, and I was like, "I need to go to the hospital *immediately*!" I was in Miami with my cousins, and they were like, "You are not dying. You are having a period." And I was like, "No. We don't have these!" Gender was always one of those complicated things where I was like, "I want to be a boy. I do not want to be a girl. Girls *suck*! I want to play football and basketball and enjoy my life." I also have a twin brother. So there were decisions made at different points in my life around what gender looks like for me in terms of expression.

Sexualitywise, I identify as pansexual, which for me means, I date some dudes, some women, and trans folk, mostly trans men. But I'm pretty picky! Gender stuff for me is complicated. I'd rather not do either one. I also live in a place where I don't feel like having a conversation about it all the time. There's a whole group of people that I work with in the Brown Boi Project, and we talk a lot about what it means to be in the middle,

and for us ourselves to be in whatever gender presentation we're in—because there's something bigger. We have other things that need to be moved, and the primary conversation doesn't need to be about gender; it needs to be about other things. So yeah, I don't know if I identify as a girl. But, you know, that's how I present. It's easiest for me to do what I need to do.

I don't actually know if I identify as a country queer. I mean, I feel like I identify as someone who is from a small zone. I feel like I identify as someone who is tied to the land. I mean, country is complicated, and it's partly based upon my own internalization. Let's just go there, right? I *hated* East Tennessee. My entire life. *Hated it.* My family is from rural Florida, and that was fine with me. When I think country, I think East Tennessee, and it took me twenty-three years to be fine with East Tennessee. Now I'm okay, but it took a long, long time. I mean, I couldn't identify as an urbanite, so I guess that's the other option—country or small town.

Here's actually how I feel—I'm able to straddle everything, and I am just as comfortable going into the country bar and doing the thing and just having a good-ass time as I am sitting at the football game, as I am being at the gay bar in the city. Like, all of it is fine. And I think that is what it means for me to be a country queer, is that you can't leave your folk at the door. You can't act like you grew up with people that weren't like the people that are acting all kinds of crazy in all kinds of ways.

And it's different! I go to New York all the time, and there's definitely a difference. I can't handle New York but for so long, and I'm like, "I got to go!" And what being queer means in New York is not what it means for me.

So now, I'm very happy with it. I wasn't for a very long time. But I'm very happy now, and one thing that I feel is really important is for other people to feel happy and rooted in who they are, and from whence they came, and to be really thankful.

E. passed away unexpectedly on September 23, 2020, following a heart surgery. E. was a brilliant, energetic force of nature who dedicated their life to organizing and uplifting many communities across the United States and the global South. E. was the executive director at PeoplesHub at the time of their passing, after spending the previous eleven years working at Highlander. They were active

with many other groups, including Black Lives Matter–Knoxville and the Black Lives of Unitarian Universalism. You can hear more of our conversation in season 1 of the Country Queers *podcast.*

E. did more than any other individual I've known to support new generations of southern and Appalachian queer, trans, and youth of color in sharpening our analysis, claiming our seats at the table, and fighting for a future in this region where each one of us can thrive.

My last communication with E. took place via email, a couple months before they passed, when I wrote to get their approval on their interview excerpt for the podcast. E. shared the following:

The only other thing I would add is that I identify as a Black, southern/Appalachian, disabled, genderqueer, pansexual, no college degree having, Unitarian Universalist "auntiemama" to three incredible nieces and nephews and four godkids. I'm 41 and I have been organizing since I was 14. Much of my work is now rooted in disability justice and spiritual fortification. As a disabled person who comes from deep spiritual and faith roots, I know we must put fortification, restoration, love, community care, wellness, and transformation at the center of all that we do. We are in a battle for humanity and for all living creatures to be seen and respected as the divine. Until we see the divine in ourselves we cannot see the divine in others. That is the work that is ahead of us and has been for generations: loving ourselves and our folks enough that we can transform this world into a place that we have never seen.

Rest in peace and power, beloved Elandria. Thank you for teaching us.

E. and me at the Appalshop Ball in Whitesburg, Kentucky, December 2017.
Photo by Oakley Fugate

Sam Gleaves at home in Berea, Kentucky, July 2016

SAM GLEAVES he/him, 20 years old

Anitsalagi (Cherokee), S'atsoyaha (Yuchi), Moneton, and Tutelo lands
Wytheville, Virginia
August 10, 2013

Sam and I first met at the 2012 STAY Summer Institute in Millpoint, West Virginia. I remember listening to his voice rising above his banjo as we sat around a campfire on a summer night in the middle of the woods. His melding of traditional and old-time mountain music with stories of queer love and defiance have brought comfort to so many Fabulachian queer people across these mountains. Sam is also the first person I ever heard use the phrase "country queer." This interview was recorded on the porch of the workshop center at the Highlander Center. Sam was a student at Berea College at the time, but he still called Wytheville, Virginia, where he was raised, home.

RAE: What do you think is the largest issue facing rural LGBTQ people?

SAM: The initial obvious one is that lack of open community. The second is lack of a history. You don't get told, "Well, there was a same-sex couple, and they lived in such and such area of the county, and they lived and farmed there for a long time together." You don't have that kind of history in stories that you get in your family and in the music, the socializing, and the visiting where we're from. You get that history in all these different places, and it makes you feel rooted here. Whereas when you discover you're queer, I think a lot of people's immediate response is to think, *Suddenly I feel like I don't belong here, when my whole life I felt I did.* There's tension between having to reconcile your queer identity with your heritage, which can seem contrary at times, like two things that can't go together. But I've found that those two things go together beautifully, and I've been able to embrace that.

I had to be in a place where both of those could be celebrated with others first, and for me that was at Berea College, because I made some friends who are country queers. We started thinking, *Well, we're fabulous and we're Appalachians, so we're Fabulachians,* and we clung to that word and used it and used it. Because it set something right in ourselves. It announced that we were fully human. That we were whole.

I have a tremendous appreciation for, and I feel a real zest in being around, other country queers. There's something about their defiance and their ability to not let the setbacks of their situation hold them down—their ability to thrive in a culture that sometimes completely embraces them

and sometimes is very hostile, in a silent, sneaky, terrible way. The sense of humor of these older country queers that I've been around is fantastic.

I have a rainbow banjo strap that I put on my banjo a couple years ago. I had some gigs coming up where I was gonna play in front of people, and I almost took it off and replaced it with just a normal leather strap before one gig. Because I thought, *This is a bunch of older folks, and I don't want to make the person I'm singing with feel uncomfortable, and I don't want to make the audience feel uncomfortable either*, because that distracts from the music, which is the holiest thing to me. I approached the person that I was gonna be singing with and I said, "Do you think that that banjo strap is too gay?" and

he said, "There's no such thing as too gay, it's like having too much money." And I was in stitches laughing. Doubled over. I thought, *I'm never taking this strap off here now*. I haven't since. So I feel most proud to be a country queer, in a way, when I put my rainbow banjo strap on and I go sing in front of people because I get to present my culture and the thing that I think is most beautiful about it—our music, our songs—and also, in a sneaky way, reveal something else about my culture: that there have *always* been queer people where I'm from and all over the world.

This interview marked the beginning of a long, dear friendship between Sam and me. I just adore him, and want to hug him and hold on tight every time I see him.

My early list of questions for Country Queers interviews was very focused on what was challenging in our experiences. I still vividly remember, at the end of our interview, that Sam suggested I add in questions about joy, humor, and fun. You can find more of Sam's story, and a follow-up conversation we recorded nearly ten years later, in season 2 of the podcast.

Dandelion, Western Massachusetts, 2023. Photo by Vick Quezada

"FRANCES" she/her, 78 years old

Nipmuc, Pocumtuc, and Muhhekunneuw (Mohican) lands
Western Massachusetts
September 2013

In September 2013, a college friend put me in touch with a queer elder living in a small town in western Massachusetts. I met "Frances" (a pseudonym I created because she did not want to be photographed or identified by name) downtown. She walked me across the street to a bar and grill on Main Street. I recall her using a walker. She was short and adorable, sporting a red flannel shirt and jeans, and she ate French onion soup during our interview. She was feisty as hell and had a gravelly laugh that punctuated her stories.

FRANCES: I'm Frances, and I'm seventy-eight, and I live in Massachusetts. And I read your— what do you call this, a blog or what? Okay. I have a few suggestions. Number one, I was born this way and I've lived this way all my life—pretty successfully, I think, without too much trouble. And when there was any kind of trouble, I kind of ignored it, and it went away. I realize that doesn't always happen. During my working career, I lost two jobs because of being gay. I prefer "gay" to "queer," and that was another thing I was gonna tell you: that word goes against me, really hard, probably because of my age.

When I grew up that was a horrible, dirty word. In my day, they used "queer" a lot, but now they don't. You rarely hear it—unless they say it behind my back, which, I don't care. And there's a thing there too: you have to become a little bit hardened, and you have to decide, *I'm gonna live a certain way*, but you have to live this way decently. You can't live it like a flaming nut.

Another thing I was going to suggest: no matter where you go, even to your hometown, do not go in there and say, "Here I am. I'm gay. Line up to kiss my behind!" Do not do that, because that'll kill you right away. And you don't need to do that. Just live. Be the person you are, and everybody will either accept you or not, and the ones that don't will just go away. That's my experience, and that's mostly the way it has happened.

I was born April 6, 1935, in Cold Brook, New Hampshire, but I grew up in Russell, which is about four miles down the road. I gave my mother a lot of trouble, too, with the birthing and labor pains and all of that. She told me I was terrible. My father was French Canadian. He came from Norton, Vermont, and was part Abenaki Indian. He educated himself on the farm. He was a master electrician, and he did it all by home study. My mother was a hometown girl from Russell, a homemaker, although in her later years she did go to work, when the nest became empty and she needed something to do. I went to a local school.

I was in a convent for seven years. It was a teaching order, and I left for two reasons. One, I'm not a teacher, and they couldn't find anything else for me to do. Teaching just drove me crazy. And then . . . being gay was like being a kid in a candy store! And I fell in love, of course, but with a nun, not with God, and caused myself a lot of problems. So I decided that that was not the place to be, and I left. They told me I'd grow out of it—because I imagine there were a lot of other folks that had the same problem—but I thought I was the only one and I should get the heck out. And I did, and I'm not sorry. I was seventeen when I went in, so if I had stayed out and worked a couple of years, maybe I would have had my head on straight. But I didn't. I went right in. I already knew I was gay, but I didn't even imagine that there was a possibility of anybody living that way. I thought there was no possible way, so I decided I'd go in the convent so I'd not be bad. I was worse in there!

RAE: When did you first know you were gay?

FRANCES: I was three years old. I remember this older girl, she must have been twelve

or something, but I just thought she was so gorgeous. I followed her everywhere. She got sick of me following after her, and I got over that broken heart and went on to others! But I never had a real close encounter until after I was out of the convent. Although we did get kinda friendly in there—with the person I was crazy about—but that's not very nice for me to talk about.

RAE: Did you come out to your family when you were young?

FRANCES: No! No, no, no! You didn't talk about it! And you hoped it would go away, because nobody else was gay in that town, that I knew of then. It was seen as a terrible thing, and there were jokes, so you didn't want to let anybody know. I think my mother knew, but she didn't ask me until after I came out of the convent. By that time I was twenty-four, and I told her yes. Mainly because I had met some people who were, through my brother-in-law, who is kind of a redneck. He didn't realize. I think he does now, but we've never talked about it. And my sister and I have never talked about it, but I know she knows. I mean, how could she not? But anyway, my mother asked me not to talk to her about it, so I didn't. She said she didn't understand it, but since it was me she would accept it. My father had passed away by this time. I don't know how he would have taken that.

RAE: If you didn't want anyone to know, how did you find other gay people? Were there bars? Did you see them around?

FRANCES: It just happened that they were around, and you happened to meet. Then I found out there were bars. At the bars you could dance, and enjoy each other, and all that kind of stuff, but there was also the breakup factor there. Everybody was after somebody else, and they didn't care who it was. Relationships didn't last very long if you were a regular, 'cause there's always somebody else. If you had a roving eye, well, too bad.

RAE: How long have you been with your partner?

FRANCES: Thirty-five years. Yeah, it can be done. But you have to be compatible, interested in the same things, respect each other, and not be too possessive. I had a horse farm and a riding stable when we met. I rented out horses with another partner at the time, and we broke up, so then I was by myself. I had some good friends who were helping me out, and she happened to be in the same crowd as them. I needed help and she was willing to help, and she needed a home. It started as kind of convenience, you know? But it worked. It was never mad—well, the first five years was mad passion, but after that it cooled off, and she says now we're just two old people living together. That's it! What more do you want?

RAE: When are you happiest in your life?

FRANCES: Well, now, at seventy-eight, when I'm sitting in my own backyard, watching the grass grow, and listening to the birds. That's it! I've been in the house where I am now, and the barn, for thirty-five years, and it's getting old and rickety, just like me. Oh, I like the ocean, too.

I was a little bit . . . nervous about this all week long, but then I thought, *Oh, I'll just do it!* When you write your book, send me a copy!

I drove away from this interview sobbing. It took me a while to figure out why. I later realized it was because this was the first time in my life that I'd ever (knowingly) had a

conversation with a rural queer elder about rural queer life. Over ten years later, that emotion, born out of a scarcity of opportunity to learn from rural queer elders, has only grown. Ninety-plus interviews in, and I can count on one hand how many were elders. This is partially due to decisions I made, but it is largely due to the reality that we have been robbed of access to our rural queer elders through decades of outmigration, through the AIDS epidemic, and through the long country queer survival strategy of silence and secrecy. I will forever regret that I didn't get the chance to talk with Frances again, or to send her a copy of this book. In summer 2020, when I called the place where she'd worked, they said she had passed away.

THE ROAD TRIP

2014

Early in the spring of 2014, I borrowed a neighbor's video camera and recorded myself, with my ducks hanging out in the background, rambling about my dream of traveling around to gather rural queer oral histories. I launched a Kickstarter fundraising campaign to support a monthlong road trip in the summer, when I'd be off from work in the public schools. I honestly didn't think it would work.

But it did. The donations started pouring in, as did enthusiasm for the project. I received emails and messages from people all over what is currently known as the United States, and beyond. People in Italy and England wrote saying how much they loved the idea. Folks in Montana, Texas, Florida, Mississippi, and North Carolina invited me to their towns. I sent a mass email to every queer person I knew, reached out to LGBTQIA2S+ organizations in states I thought I might pass through, and, out of endless possibilities, a route emerged.

I spent mid-June to mid-July on the road in a used Subaru Forester with over 160,000 miles on it (and a sizeable loan). I had a flip phone and a paper atlas, a Zoom H4n audio recorder with no external mics or fancy headphones, and a Canon digital SLR camera I purchased with some of those Kickstarter funds (along with a tent, sleeping pad, and small camp stove). Covering seven thousand miles, I interviewed thirty people in thirty days. In Mississippi, Texas, New Mexico, Colorado, Kansas, and Oklahoma, I slept on the couches and floors of people who shared their stories with me. All the butches grilled for me in the summer heat. Autumn in Angleton, Texas, baked me a birthday cake and had it waiting when I arrived late on a June evening, after a long day of interviewing and driving. Autumn and her then-partner also took me to their favorite Tex-Mex restaurant, to the sno-cone stand they ran together, and down to the brown waters of the Texas Gulf where we watched seagulls fly, oil tankers float by, and people catch huge fish. People sent me on my way with homemade baked goods. They invited their friends over to meet me and share meals. I met people's parents and kids, partners and housemates, pets and livestock. Mattie, who I interviewed in Alpine, Texas, put me up for the night at the nicest hotel I'd ever stayed in—knowing I'd already been on the road nonstop for days and hadn't had much time alone. I also camped in my tent along the way. I got to visit friends in Austin and Denver on a couple days off. I took a weekend off in New Mexico—and soaked in a hot spring high up on a mountainside. I got to help Courtney in Kansas with evening goat-milking chores after our interview.

Everyone took such good care of me, in the way that country queers always do. I didn't think of it at the time, but now I bet many of the folks, particularly those older than me, were worried about me out on the road traveling solo in an old car with a flip phone. There were moments of fear on some stretches of road or in certain motel parking lots at night. I ended up sleeping in hotels more than I'd planned to, after realizing that I felt most comfortable camping alone (without my dog) if I was able to arrive in the daylight and get a sense of my surroundings and neighbors before the sun set, which long travel and interview days didn't always allow for. Since I had no GPS or smartphone, I'd spend an hour in the morning before leaving the hotel looking up Google map directions on my laptop and writing them down by

hand in my notebook. Miraculously, I didn't ever get a flat tire or break down. No one physically harassed me, and I successfully dodged all the advances of overly curious men. Somehow, I didn't even get drastically lost along the way. Someone, somewhere, was looking out for me.

I drove through thick, humid nights in Mississippi, dry, sunny days in West Texas, dramatic thunderstorms in New Mexico, glaring brightness in Colorado. I traveled mostly on two-lane highways, listening to burned CDs on repeat. Amy Ray's first country album, *Goodnight Tender*, remains the soundtrack of that trip in my memory. I still regret not stopping for a picture in the high desert of southern Colorado, where along a long stretch of flat highway with a view of the Rockies in the distance, for at least thirty miles, someone had spray-painted little black UFOs on every cow-crossing sign.

I was homesick and exhausted but also blown away, again and again, by how welcoming and vulnerable everyone was. When I arrived back home in late July, I crashed hard. I felt like I'd had an IV in my arm all month long with a strong and constant flow of other people's memories. I didn't know how to talk about the decades of other people's stories—that were somehow also our collective rural queer history—

swimming around inside my head and heart. I am an introvert, and the exhaustion at the end was *intense*.

That trip wasn't a sustainable model, but it was one of the most amazing experiences of my life. I'm incredibly grateful to each person I had the true honor of meeting along the way.

This is the longest section of the book, because of the abundance of interviews gathered in that time. In the early days, I'd interview anyone who got in touch wanting to share their story, so most interviews were gathered in those first two years. In the pages ahead, you'll meet ten people I interviewed that month. Several of the excerpts include accounts of traumatic events and experiences, including threats and realities of physical violence and death from HIV/AIDS. You'll notice that two of the excerpts are significantly longer than the others, to allow space for accounts of broader historical events and contexts.

Mason and Kilo in the "bar" she built at home, southern Mississippi, June 2014

MASON MICHAEL she/her, 58 years old

Mvskoke (Muscogee) and Chahta (Choctaw) lands
Southern Mississippi
June 19–20, 2014

Mason reached out to me after the Kickstarter campaign made it onto her radar. She invited me down to interview her and her partner, Catherine, at their home. Mason told me she'd pick me up in her truck at the end of their road, and I kept thinking, I grew up on a rough gravel mountain road, I'll be fine! *I felt hesitant, so far from home, to leave my car somewhere and get picked up by a stranger to stay with them overnight. Mason was the second interview on the trip, and she and Catherine were the first to host me in their home.*

But I immediately felt comfortable in their house, which Mason had built. It sat high up on stilts, a quirky, semi-finished pastiche. The kitchen and living room—where we recorded interviews and where I slept—was a beautifully finished room, cooled by a window-mounted air conditioner. Walking out the back door, you'd cross a stretch of deck to another air-conditioned, finished room, which was their bedroom. I remember a shotgun hanging on the wall by a rainbow strap, and I still wish I had taken a picture of it.

MASON: I was born in Pensacola, Florida, and I was a Navy brat. My mother was from Pensacola, and all her kinfolk were there. So that's where I call home. We moved all over the world, which gave me an opportunity to see the world. But I always wanted to live in the country. I don't know if I inherited that from my grandfather or what. He would've rather been out in the woods than in the suburbs or in the city, and that's what I always dreamed of, having a place in the country, especially on a creek.

We created our own queer history up in Ovett, Mississippi, in 1993. Wanda and Brenda Henson purchased 120 acres outside of Hattiesburg, with the intention of using that for a lesbian campground and to hold our annual women's music festivals. We called it Camp Sister Spirit.

I worked the Gulf Coast Women's Music and Comedy Festival every year. It started in 1989, and it went on until about 2005. In '93, me and my girlfriend had just broken up, and the March on Washington was the next week.* So I said, "I'm out of here, I'm going to Washington." After the march, I stayed with Wanda and Brenda for a couple weeks. Sister Spirit Incorporated was already a nonprofit

---

* For more on the 1993 March on Washington for Lesbian, Gay and Bi Equal Rights and Liberation, see Jeffery Schmalz, "March for Gay Rights; Gay Marchers Throng Mall in Appeal for Rights," *New York Times*, April 26, 1993, https://www.nytimes.com/1993/04/26/us/march-for-gay-rights-gay-

organization that they had on the coast over at Gulfport, Mississippi. They ran a food bank and had meetings for women—a lot of consciousness raising and stuff like that—and the Gulf Coast Women's Festival was born out of that. While I was staying with them, I met a woman who lived in North Carolina, so I went up there and stayed for several months and worked on an old farmhouse she had up there. And that's when I got the call from Wanda and Brenda. They said, "We got the land. We need you to come home."

So I left North Carolina and come back to the land in Ovett. It was 120 acres on a creek. There's five acres of grapes, there's a bunch of pink barns. There were several buildings on the property: an old deer stand, a big old barn that we converted into a meeting space, and libraries and offices and a commercial kitchen. We ran a big food kitchen up there, too. We fed about four hundred families a month out of the food bank up there. We'd take their food boxes down the driveway and meet them at the gate. We didn't let everybody up. Not that we had anything to hide, but people were too curious and it's just not their business. We didn't want everyone to know exactly how everything was set

up there. We didn't even have to advertise; word just got out. When they found out we were up there, people called us for help. They knew we were there to help people, and it just snowballed.

We had several festivals right there on the land. Three thousand women from all over the world came through there during that time. We had a bunch of people there that didn't even speak English for a while. It was really a lot of fun. Everybody added their ideas to it, their art projects, and everybody volunteered to build a fence around the property. Me, Wanda, and Brenda were the main people. Pam came and lived there, and there was another woman, Kathy. Basically, there was never more than about four or five of us living there, permanently, at one time.

RAE: When did stuff start getting crazy? When did people start messing with you?

MASON: It was October or November, I guess, when we found the dog on the mailbox. We walked out one morning to check the mail and there was a dead dog draped over our little mailbox with bullet holes in it. The mailbox was stuffed with bloody tampons

marchers-throng-mall-in-appeal-for-rights.html; "Reflections on the 1993 March on Washington," National LGBTQ Task Force, April 25, 2013, www.thetaskforce.org/news/reflections-on-the-1993-march-on-washington.

and had a sign on it, "Get out of here, bitches." Something like that.

They tried to run us off the road. They'd sit outside and fire shots across our property and set off big bombs that would just rattle everything in the house. It's two thousand feet off the road, so you know those were some powerful acetylene bombs. Day and night. They'd come down to our driveway, cut donuts, hooting and hollering, shooting their guns, and honking their horns. We put mirrors up all across the front to throw their energy back to them, and as soon as we did, the first truck that came down there slid off the road, jabbed up against the pine tree. There were three guys in it. One of them got out, and he went running back to the store up the road. The other two idiots come walking up to the middle of the camp with a great big gun with a scope on it. One of them comes clomping up our driveway. Well, by then he's got three or four guns trained on him 'cause we got him surrounded. Wanda walked up to him, and she thinks she's the one that disarmed him with her talk, but she don't realize I was sitting there with a .30-30 rifle aimed right on his head.

We took him in, and he tried to make some phone calls to get somebody to come get him. Nobody would come get him, so me and Pam, we loaded him up in her truck.

We took his gun from him, unloaded it, and put it in the rifle rack. We put the other two guys in the back of the truck, and we go driving up to the little store where all the local guys hang out. We get out of the truck and we're handing the guys back their guns. And a guy runs up, and he says, "Oh, man, look what happened." He pulls his shirt up, and he's got this big old rip across his belly, and I looked at him and said, "How'd you do that?" And he said, "Ran into that damn barbed wire fence when I was running." I said, "What the fuck are you doing on my barbed wire fence?" And his eyes got so big 'cause he didn't realize me and Pam were the women from the camp! He thought we were two other guys from somewhere. So we got out of the truck and started talking with all the guys. Turns out they were finishers. I was a carpenter, and we worked on a bunch of the same jobs. We had so much in common, and before it was over with, I go, "Hey, we'll come help you build that place that just come on."

RAE: When did it get to where there was all this national attention?

MASON: How did that start? That story about the dog hit the paper, and next thing you know, it just blew up. Wanda knows how to use the press, and she has a lot of contacts. It didn't take long for the word to get out. We had reporters from everywhere coming in. Wanda wanted everyone to know, 'cause if they didn't, we'd be dead. We had to let everybody know: "We're here. This is going on. Keep an eye on it."

RAE: Once the media came, did things get worse? Did things get better?

MASON: Oh, it stirred up the local people more that were already against us. It gave them more provocation, I guess, to go against us. In the gay community, it got a lot of people interested. A lot of people came and got involved because of that.

RAE: Who was it in Mississippi who was fighting against you? Local politicians, or—

MASON: Oh, yeah, God—it went all the way up to the governor. We had senators, we had congressmen who would shut down the town. They raffled off shotguns to get money in order to sue us to get us off our property. They wanted us gone. They kept offering to buy it. We told them, "Yeah, we'll sell it to you for $1 million. And we'll go build ten more of them. Go ahead and buy it." They wouldn't buy it.

RAE: Wow! Then I was reading in one of those articles you showed me about gunshots?

MASON: Yeah. It was constant, gunshots and shooting around the perimeter. That's why we put those big fences up, so at least they couldn't see us. We'd build a fence; they'd build a deer stand. We'd build a higher fence; they'd build a higher deer stand.

RAE: And it went on for three years?

MASON: Mm-hmm.

RAE: Wow. You want to talk about the *Jerry Springer Show*?

MASON: That was just a mess. It was an ambush. The whole thing was set up. They had Wanda so worked up and confused. She lost her cool, and because of that a lot of gay people dropped the whole thing. They thought she was just a total nutcase.

RAE: What was the scene like in there?

MASON: The producers had us in there an hour before the show even started, and they had our enemies sitting across the aisle from us. They had us worked up to where we were

almost flinging chairs at each other by the time they started filming.

When we did *Jerry Springer*—he was just coming off a show like [*Phil*] *Donahue*—a serious talk show. We were under the impression that's what this would be like. But instead, this was the first show where he went renegade. They tried to get us to physically fight, and none of us would. It was just a fiasco.

RAE: So things eventually died down, and nobody ever got hurt?

MASON: No one was ever shot. They knew better than to shoot anybody, 'cause Robin Tyler was lined up and she was ready. She wanted to bring Queer Nation in and march. But we prevented her from doing that because we have to live here. We've got to deal with these people, and it ain't fair for the ones who weren't involved to turn everything into a circus. But if they'd have shot somebody, you damned sure bet there'd have been a million queers descended on Ovett. They knew that. They weren't that stupid.

RAE: You said somebody set a car on fire at one point?

MASON: Yeah, they tried to set a car on fire and roll it down the hill to set our land on fire, and that's when we had the forest department come out and cut us a fire break all the way around our property.

RAE: Wow. It sounds like it was stressful. Was it scary?

MASON: Not to me. I mean, it was to a lot of people. I don't know, maybe I should've been, but I wasn't scared. I've been around these rednecks long enough they don't scare me. They're big shits in a group, they all think they're real good. But anytime I met one of them one on one, or even one on two, they're chickenshits. They wouldn't deal with you one on one. They got to have their little gang. I was always armed. I wasn't afraid of them.

* For more on Robin Tyler, see https://www.robintyler.com. For a brief history of Queer Nation, see Caitlin Donohue, "When Queer Nation 'Bashed Back' against Homophobia with Street Patrols and Glitter," KQED, June 3, 2019, https://www.kqed.org/arts/13858167/queer-nation-lgbtq-activism-90s.

I had never heard of Camp Sister Spirit before meeting Mason, or the Gulf Coast Women's Festival, or even Queer Nation or the 1993 March on Washington for Lesbian, Gay and Bi Equal Rights and Liberation. When I read through this interview in fall 2023, after an intense escalation of legislative and physical attacks on LGBTQIA2S+ spaces in the past six months alone, I get goosebumps thinking about the necessity of queer oral histories. Reading this story, I'm reminded about the ways rural queer people have been robbed of our elders, and how this disconnection has created lasting harm, leaving us more vulnerable and less prepared for attacks from the far right.

I am so grateful to Mason for teaching me about this history of radical lesbians in Mississippi in the 1990s, and to Catherine for feeding me and welcoming me into their home. I still think often and fondly of their peaceful refuge in the woods and swamps of southern Mississippi.

Mason Michael (first from right) and others at Camp Sister Spirit, Ovett, Mississippi, 1994 or 1995. Photo courtesy of Mason Michael

Sandra Vera (left) and April Vera (right) outside their home, Lake Jackson, Texas, June 2014

SANDRA VERA she/her, 43 years old

Karankawa, Tap Pilam Coahuiltecan, and Esto'k Gna (Carrizo/Comecrudo) lands
Lake Jackson, Texas
June 20, 2014

If I remember correctly, I got connected to Sandra through the unparalleled lesbian phone (or, in this case, email) tree. I think my friend in Texas put me in touch with a friend of hers in Florida, who put me in touch with an older lesbian in middle Tennessee, and someone else in Texas who put me in touch with Sandra. Anyway, it is a fact that lesbians pre-internet were impressively well connected and organized via snail mail newsletters and phone trees. Sandra and her wife, April, were incredibly sweet to me. I think they probably thought I was a bit crazy to be out on this trip (which was true). I will always be grateful to Sandra for rescuing me from the nest of fire ants I stepped into in sandals while making a picture of them on their front porch.

SANDRA: It's a very Christian-oriented town, Lake Jackson is. We've got what we call Church Alley. People for the most part are friendly. It's near the coast. That's about it! Not a whole heck of a lot going on in Lake Jackson.

I identify as a lesbian. My whole life I've been a tomboy, but I've never identified as a boy. The very first person I ever told that I was gay was my best friend, Rhonda, who I grew up with. She is also our roommate, but she's not here today. It wasn't until high school, when I was probably sixteen or seventeen, when people close to me knew. My sister was like, "I already knew." My brother never expressed any type of opinion about it at all. He and my sister-in-law have always been very accepting of my girlfriends. I was Dad's shadow, so if he got in his truck to go to the dump, I was in the truck going with him. If he was working on the roof, I was beside him working on the roof. I think he might not have been so surprised.

I work mostly with men. There's only one other woman that's a technician in my block. The men that I work with, 90 percent of them are Christian, conservative, hunting, fishing, good old boys. I seem to fit in with them, though. It took a while for them to get used to me being around. I was obviously out. I didn't have anything to hide. At first, I didn't feel like I was very respected by them. First of all, you're a female in the workplace where— it's a boy's club in there. But now it's a totally different feeling, nine years later. I've been working with those same guys, and they're like brothers now, and being gay, being a woman in that workplace—it's fine for me. I haven't had any issues.

The plant that I work at is one of the leading chemical manufacturers in the world. It's a German-based company, and at our particular site we make over twenty-two different products. I work in the heart of the whole plant, which is the utilities department. In the department, we have pressure steam and distribute it throughout the whole plant in a cogeneration unit. A cogeneration unit not only makes this high-pressure steam, but the byproduct of it is electricity, so it makes eighty-five megawatts of electricity. All the plants also have a wastewater stream that comes to us. It's either high or low PH, or real acidic, alkaline. We'll take it, and we'll treat it to the specifications of the state and governmental regulations. The other aspects are making deionized [DI] water and keeping up with the infrastructure of the plant as far as the pipelines, the river water, the potable water, the DI water from gate to gate, the whole plant.

RAE: Cool! I don't know what most of that means.

SANDRA: Makes for a long day is what it means.

RAE: Did you ever know about any gay people in the area when you were growing up here?

SANDRA: When I was probably five years old,

my dad . . . he worked in the chemical plant too, but he also did side jobs. And he cut the grass for these two older women who lived together. I was always very interested in the dynamic there, and if he was going to mow their yard, I was going. I wanted to be around them. There was something that attracted me to them. But I don't think they ever were out as a couple. It seems like I vaguely remember my parents talking about it. But as far as the other people that I've known throughout my life who were much older than me that I knew were gay, or suspected of being gay, they were not out. There was an older lady from this area who was married to a man just to be married to a man, but she was lesbian. And she said, "I married him because that's what I was supposed to do." So we've existed around here, but I think long ago was a lot harder to be out and open about it.

I probably only spent two or three hours with Sandra and April, but I remember laughing a lot, and wishing I lived closer 'cause they seemed like people who knew how to have a good country time (boats! four-wheelers! dogs!). I love how Sandra describes not feeling

tension or conflict around her sexuality in relation to her local community. Sandra is one of the narrators whose stories disprove the pervasive stereotype that rural queer people's lives tend to be full of harassment and violence. Across differences in gender, race, and ethnicity, many people told me that they haven't had significant issues in their towns and that their communities mostly treat them well. In the beginning of this project, my questions skewed heavily toward asking what issues and challenges rural queer people faced, but many narrators, including Sandra, taught me that those weren't necessarily the right questions to ask and that our struggles aren't the only interesting or important things to talk about.

David Rodriguez in Laura Freeman's yard, Austin, Texas, June 2014

DAVID RODRIGUEZ he/him, 26 years old

Jumanos, Tonkawa, Ndé Kónitsąąíí Gokíyaa (Lipan Apache),
Sana, and Tap Pilam Coahuiltecan lands
Bastrop, Texas
June 22, 2014

After seven long days on the road, I took a couple days off in Austin. My friend Laura Freeman hosted a brunch at her house so I could visit with friends while passing through. She invited David to the meal, thinking we'd enjoy meeting each other. I was already real tired and overwhelmed by my jam-packed interview schedule for the three weeks ahead. But, after chatting with David, I couldn't turn down the chance to interview him. We sat at a patio table surrounded by Laura's yard full of Texas wildflowers with cats, dogs, and chickens trotting by. David lived a ways out of town in Bastrop at the time. This interview was transcribed by my ex-turned-longtime-friend, Riley Cockrell.

DAVID: I grew up near a small town called Wharton, Texas, population: 10,000 people. It's very agriculturally oriented. When I was growing up, it was all about rice, corn, and cotton. It's been said that our county produces more rice than the entire nation of China, but that's changed because of the water crisis in Texas. So now the industry is almost completely dead.

I grew up outside of town. We had two acres and a house that we lived in for a long time. I had goats when I was younger. I was part of FFA [Future Farmers of America], raised animals for the fair, and sold them every year at auction. I loved it. I raised hogs, show pigs for two years, and then a heifer for one. So my first experience with agriculture was very corporate ag—but still, it was part of the culture.

I grew up in a very Tejano-type home here in Texas. My family has been in Texas longer than Texas has been a state. So I still had a Hispanic upbringing, but not so much of an identifier as being from Mexico as being Tejano. That was a big part of my childhood. My mother and father split up when I was younger, so then it just became my mother and me, and my younger siblings. She was eighteen when she had me, so we kind of grew up together. Having a younger mom is great because you can experience everything together, and be very open and honest with each other about things. Now, my mother is my best friend in the entire world.

She was a single mom until she got with her new husband my senior year in high school. He was a very far-right conservative Christian, and his previous wife had left him for another woman, so he was really resentful toward gays in general. I remember on Halloween of 2005, my mom asked me if I was gay. I had promised myself that I would be honest if she asked me. At first, she said, "Are you gay?" And I was like, "Yes, I'm always happy." Then she was like, "That's not the question I'm asking you." Her next question was, "Do you like having sex with men?" And my answer was, "Yes, I do."

I was seventeen at the time. She said, "You have sixty seconds to get out of the house, and if you don't, I'm going to hit you with his baseball bat," and she went and got a baseball bat. There wasn't any option of staying at home. So I left. And I walked. And I have never felt freer than I did that very moment that I walked out of that house. I made a promise to myself that day, walking to the gas station, that I would never hide who I am for anyone ever again, and I've stayed true to that. I'm very honest and open about who I am, and what I do, and what I believe in.

My mother and I had a horrible relationship after that, for six months. We hated each other and were argumentative and fighting all the time. I didn't live with her anymore, and was living with whoever I could live with. I just hopped around houses. I stayed with my uncle sometimes or my grandparents or other people—my dad. I almost didn't graduate high school, but finally got done with school, graduated, got out of there, left, and went to college. That year was a pretty rough time.

But my mom finally has come around, and now it's not even an issue at all. She kind of started coming along on her own and realizing that the things being taught at church weren't necessarily what she agreed with. Recently, I asked her about how she felt that day, and did she have hate in her heart, or was it anger? She said it was neither; it was disappointment. That was the first time that I ever asked her how she felt about it, and to hear that it was disappointment, and it wasn't anger and it wasn't hate. It was just driven by religious fanatics who said she needed to do whatever she had to do to protect her other children. So it took her growing and realizing that I'm still the same person, and she's just relaxed a lot in life, and realized that she doesn't need to take things so hard and so personal. It just doesn't matter anymore.

RAE: What do you think the largest issue facing your community is?

DAVID: I'm a huge environmentalist, and I think the biggest issue facing communities in Texas is environmental, because the state government is allowing industries to come in and completely destroy our communities.

They're bringing in fracking industries, they're bringing in petroleum-processing facilities, they're bringing in pipe building. What they're trying to sell to all of us is that they're increasing jobs and wealth, but in actuality, we're losing the things that we love the most out in the country. We're losing our resources. Our aquifers are drying up. Our rivers are drying up.

I come from a county where we have 13 percent unemployment. The entire rice-farming industry has been destroyed because there isn't enough water. So a county that's subsisted on rice farming is now within three years of having to completely shift its economy, yet they're allowing the fracking industry to come in and use up all the water that it wants. That's a huge problem facing our community. It doesn't matter whether you're gay, Black, straight, white; we're all going to be needing water. We're all going to be needing food. And when these industries come in and completely destroy the places where we live. . . . We're all equal when the end result is extinction.

RAE: What do you think is the biggest issue facing queer people right now?

DAVID: A big issue facing queers right now is this whole idea of normalization, this idea of wanting to live this heteronormative lifestyle where people want to be like straight people, and I think the marriage equality movement has really taken up that "we want to be like everyone else" kind of thing. To me, that's not what being gay is about. I know that I'm different. I know that gay people are different, and we should accept and embrace that difference.

RAE: Is there anything you'd want to say to other rural queer people out there?

DAVID: I think what I want to say to other rural queer people—because this is something that I've thought for a long time would be great to hear—is: you are not alone.

There are other people just like you out there. So many times, people feel like they're the only one. And they're not. There are other people who want to live in the country, who are rural, who are queer, and that's what you need to know: you are not the only one. There are others of us.

At some point during our conversation I said to David, "I wish West Virginia and Texas were closer!" Because so much of the way he talked about his dreams for his future were resonant for me. Every time I come across data showing that LGBTQIA2S+ youth experience significantly higher rates of houselessness and housing insecurity than their straight and cis peers, I think of his coming-out story. There's something beautiful in this story of the evolution in David's relationship with his mother. I also appreciate the way David's story demonstrates the complex layers of belonging we navigate as rural queer people. His belonging to the land has never been questioned, but his ability to experience belonging within his own family was deeply contested in his high school years. Since the time of our interview in 2013, David and his husband have moved back to the part of Texas where David was raised. They run a dairy goat farm called Country Q's (!), selling soap, candles, and salves at area farmers markets and stores. You can hear more of his interview in season 1 of the Country Queers *podcast.*

Allie Gartman in downtown Big Spring, Texas, June 2014

ALLIE GARTMAN she/they, 19 years old

Kiikaapoi (Kickapoo), Ndé Kónitsąąíí Gokíyaa (Lipan Apache),
Nʉmʉnʉʉ (Comanche), and Jumanos lands
Big Spring, Texas
June 23, 2014

After seeing the project's Kickstarter, Allie invited me to Big Spring to interview her. I left Austin that morning and drove through wide expanses of the Texas hill country. As I drove on, the land got flatter, and constellations of windmills rose like surreal groves of enormous, futuristic trees. Closer to Big Spring, the windmill groves gave way to endless seas of pumpjacks—slow, rusted, top-heavy dinosaurs incessantly pumping oil out of the earth. Allie and I met up on the patio of a café downtown and recorded a short interview. Afterward, we walked around town while I made pictures.

Allie told me that Big Spring was in the middle of a new oil boom. New trailer parks were popping up on the edge of town to house workers; schools were overflowing with new students, unable to hire teachers fast enough to keep up; and rent was through the roof. But she also said elders in town were expressing concerns already for what would happen when this next boom turned to bust. "We gotta think about the future," she said. "What happens when the oil is gone? When the oil dries up, what're we gonna do with all this stuff?" This interview was transcribed by Heidi Marsh.

ALLIE: Big Spring is pretty quiet. Not a whole lot goin' on. It's pretty dry. Pretty hot most of the time. Everybody knows everybody, and everybody helps everybody. It's just a very average little sleepy West Texas town. I was born here in Big Spring, but I've lived in Alpine, Texas. I've lived in Bullhead City, Arizona. I've lived in Longview, Texas. My mom kept getting promoted in her job, so we moved back and forth between places, but now that I'm grown up, I came back here for college.

Growing up was pretty normal, I guess. I just had a pretty average childhood. I had pets, I liked the color pink, I liked different Barbie dolls . . . stuff like that.

I identify as pansexual, which to me means that I don't base who I like, sexually, on their perceived gender. I knew I wasn't straight probably when I was six or seven, just because I found something pretty in everybody. But the way I found out was actually watching *The Rocky Horror Picture Show* for the first time. And when Tim Curry came out in drag, I just—I don't know. In the back of my head I was like *Wow! That's really attractive. I like that. I think that's hot.* And it just startled me. I was like, *Okay, where did that thought come from?* So I just kinda thought about it for a minute. I stopped the movie, and I went over to the computer and I started looking online. I came across "pansexual," and I started reading the definition, and I was like, *Oh my God, this is me! This is how I feel. This is who I am.*

RAE: How old were you?

ALLIE: I was probably about twelve or thirteen at that time.

RAE: Did you have a lot of other queer friends in high school?

ALLIE: Yeah. I hung out with the artsy kids, the nerds, the weird kids, you know? Some of us were more out than others, but everybody just kind of knew that's the group of kids that . . . aren't straight. They're the queer ones, they're the weird ones.

RAE: Do you think that living in smaller towns made it harder to come out than if you had lived in the city? Do you think the experience would have been different?

ALLIE: Yeah. Mostly just because of what I said before: everybody knows everybody here. Like, I can't even sneeze at the grocery store without my grandma finding out about it and asking me if I feel sick. As soon

as I think about doing something, someone already knows and is telling somebody else, and it's just all over before I even finished what I'm doing. So it is a lot harder, mostly because of that mentality. But also just . . . especially in the South, it's still the Bible Belt. It's still a lot of fire and damnation and hell and *queers are gonna burn in hell for all eternity*, you know? That we're just . . . we're not right, we're not natural. And growing up hearing that *does* make a lot of people afraid to come out, just 'cause they don't want that hate from their friends and family and neighbors and coworkers and people around town.

RAE: When are you most proud to be, like, country? Or are you?

ALLIE: When I go out of state and people compliment me on my manners and how polite I am, just how well mannered I am. They're like, "You're from the South, aren't you?" and I'm like, "Yes. Yes, I am. I'm from Texas." And they're like, "Mm-hmm, we should have known. You're so polite and well mannered." And I'm just like, *Yay, my parents did something right!*

RAE: When are you the happiest in your life?

ALLIE: I'm just generally a happy person. I'm happy most of the time. But I'd have to say I'm the happiest when I'm working. I deliver the local newspaper, and one of my routes is pretty long. It takes about an hour and a half to do the route, and it's a lot of alone time out in the middle of nowhere, out in the country part of town, out in the boondocks. I get a lot of time to think and contemplate things, listen to music and just relax and not have to stress about anything. Just drive and relax.

RAE: Do you feel pressure to move to a city?

ALLIE: No. I feel pretty comfortable here. I just go about my day-to-day activities, and it's a pretty boring, average life. I wake up, I go to class, I go get my papers, I go to work, I go back to my dorm, I do homework, play around on the computer, go to sleep, wake up, do it all over again. That's just a typical day for me. So, I don't feel pressured to move to a big city. Maybe I would like to move to a big city just for more to do? Just 'cause I'm that kinda person? Maybe. But we do have Midland and Odessa, about half an hour away, an hour away. And . . . they're big cities, I guess you could technically say. They have stuff to do.

When I was growing up, my reference point for a city was my dad's hometown of Fort Wayne, Indiana. I remember driving through downtown, mouth and nose pressed against the window, fogging it up with my breath as I stared up at those tall buildings, the first skyscrapers I'd ever seen. Since leaving West Virginia, I've been fortunate to visit cities across the country and world, where even the smallest skyscrapers dwarf those Fort Wayne buildings. But, the moment when Allie describes Odessa and Midland as big cities feels so intensely familiar and incredibly endearing to me, and Allie's youthfulness adds an important voice to this collection.

Out of all the towns I passed through on that road trip, Big Spring felt the most like home—not in terms of architecture or landscape, but in terms of some universal flavor of towns built around extractive industries. The histories of boom and bust, environmental ravagement, and intense and dangerous physical jobs all painted across the face of Big Spring reminded me of West Virginia. I took countless photos of a long-abandoned storefronts downtown.

Computers from the early nineties gathered dust on uncleared desks covered in papers. A sticker on a window read "We Believe in Big Spring," and I felt the familiar ache in my chest of abiding love for small towns that have seen better days, that deserve so much more, that are trying to find their way into a future beyond extraction of coal, oil, or gas.

Crisosto Apache at home in their backyard, Denver, Colorado, June 2014

CRISOSTO APACHE they/them, 42 years old

Núuchi-u (Ute), Tsitsistas (Cheyenne), Ndé Kónitsąąíí Gokíyaa
(Lipan Apache), and Hinono'eiteen (Arapaho) lands
Denver, Colorado
June 28, 2014

I connected with Crisosto before I left West Virginia on the road trip, after coming across the Two Spirit National Cultural Exchange, an organization they founded and directed, online. We had several phone calls, and I planned my route so that I'd make sure to catch Crisosto in Denver before they left for a trip back home to the Mescalero Apache Reservation in New Mexico. We sat down at their kitchen table in a bright, airy house. Over the course of the afternoon, their partner, mother, and nephews all came in and out of the kitchen. The clock on the wall announced the hour through bird calls. This interview was transcribed by Montanna Mills.

CRISOSTO: It's customary that I introduce myself in my native language, so I'm gonna do that. *Shí'taí k'an dé, nił'daagut'é. Shí Crisosto Apache húún'zhyé'. Shi Mashgalénde áan'sht'ííd.* What I basically said is: Hello, my name is Crisosto Apache, and I'm Mescalero Apache. I'm forty-two, and I currently live in Denver, but I'm originally from the Mescalero Apache Reservation in New Mexico.

I was born and raised on the Mescalero Apache Reservation. I originally grew up with my father, who was Diné, Navajo. When I was really young, I remember staying with him a little bit, and he was from To'hajiilee, formerly known as Cañoncito, outside of Albuquerque. After a while, he ended up taking me back to my mom's, in Mescalero.

On the reservation, we moved around a little bit, because it's really vast and huge. The area that I grew up in is between seven and eight thousand feet, up in the mountains. There was a forest, and we used to run around and play in the forest. But growing up on the reservation is a very interesting experience, and it's taken me a long time to realize the significance of being Native American, being two-spirit, and also having an education, which is really kind of unique to my family.

There's this whole idea called historical trauma. It's the transmission of intergenerational trauma that a lot of Native Americans have dealt with. From forced removal from their lands, to massacres, to the school systems, to starvation, to internment camps—whatever, you name it. All of that plays into my history, and it plays into a lot of Native American history.

It was difficult growing up because my mom had separated from my father and then remarried to my stepfather, who's currently still in the house. We were sort of a poor family. The highest level of education my parents had was tenth grade. They both dropped out. My stepfather had some experience working trades, so whatever work he could get as a tradesman is what he did. They both have a lot of experience in silversmithing, so they made jewelry on the side to supplement the income. My mother worked as a dietician when I was a lot younger. But then, because we moved around a lot, she ended up having to take care of us.

My older brother is from a different parent; there's me and my little brother, from my mom and my father; there's two stepsisters, who were from my stepfather's previous marriage; and then there's my two sisters, from their marriage now. So we grew up, off and on, with a huge family. And I'm sure that was really hard, to raise that many kids, on the level of education that he had, and for whatever jobs they could get. At the time, I didn't understand that, but now that I'm older, and now that I'm raising my nephews, I realize what it takes to raise a family. To be financially responsible for them, to be emotionally responsible for them, and all of these things that parents go through. I've been thrown into that within a

year. We grew up with very little money, but we managed.

I always knew, my whole life, that I was gay. From a very young age, I was very curious about it, but I didn't understand it. And in the back of my mind, I always wondered if people were all like that. I started to see that there was this behavior that was happening where guys and girls got together, and that was dating. But I never did see girls and girls, or guys and guys—in any of the relationships that I observed, on or off the reservation.

However, while I was growing up, I remember seeing some guys dress up as women on my reservation. And I knew who they were, and the community knew who they were. There's a heavy debate in Native American communities about how much of that is real, and how much of that is part of our culture. From all the research that I've done on two-spirit people and reservation communities—and all the elders that I've talked to, who are very traditional—I've learned that, culturally, that behavior was accepted within the community because it had a function. There was a spiritual function; there was a communal function. And we don't disown our people, we don't disown our families, and everybody has a purpose. Those are some of the basic teachings within our culture.

Within the culture itself, these people are given responsibilities. They might not fit the responsibilities that straight people have, such as procreation, providing for the family. But in terms of the way they operated within the community, there was a purpose for them, and in some societies and some cultures, because of how that balance is integrated within one person, a lot of these communities saw that as a gift, because of how we describe the universe around us. There's a male universe and a female universe, and there's a sense of balance that allows them to interact with each other. Our seasons are male and female. Our directions are male and female. Our environments are male and female. Even the rain—there's a male rain and a female rain.

Now, growing up, however, there has been this conflict that I've inherited in terms of Western thought and Western religion, and how much guilt and shame was pushed on a lot of Native people for practicing their culture. That is something that I see a lot of people struggle with still. It's that integration of fundamental religion, and how much damage that has done, and continues to do, to Native communities.

But growing up, there were people within our community who were able to express themselves the way they do, and there isn't any shame in presenting yourself that way. But I was still confused. I went to a public school off the reservation, and I did my own research in terms of what I thought I was, and I started hearing from other people and the way they talked, the derogatory terms, like "faggot," "gay," "sissy." I started finding out what these terms meant and that they weren't nice. So I started to internalize a lot of that, and I was like, *Who I am, and what I am, I can't tell anybody, because it's "wrong."*

When I was seventeen, I went back home, and I was in the kitchen with my mother. We were doing dishes, and something in the back of my mind said, *I need to tell my mother. I need to tell my mom what is going on.* So I told her I was gay. She told me, "You know what? You're my son. You live your life how you were born into. There's nothing you can do to change that. All I care is that you're happy, and that you take care of yourself. I'm still your mother, this is still your family, and you're still my son. Nothing has changed."

It wasn't until later—after I came out again as a two-spirit person—that I found out that she was not happy. Not because I was gay; it was because I had had a disconnection to my culture. So when I came out and found the term "two-spirit" and realized that there was a cultural part of my identity, which is what I felt was missing all these years—even though I told myself I was gay and was living in a gay way, there was still something missing. It wasn't until I discovered the term "two-spirit," and that was closest to whatever it is I was looking for, was wanting to put back. It was that connection to my culture, that connection to my language, that connection to my creation stories, that connection to my family and to my community. My heritage. My lineage. All of that.

Once I started to understand that, I went back home, and I started integrating myself back into my culture, my language. I started including my cultural aspects in my identity. And I told my mom, "I remember telling you I was gay a long time ago. Do you remember that?" She says, "Yeah." And I was like, "Well, I don't think I'm gay. I think I'm a two-spirit person." And she said, "Well, what's that?" I said, "It's somebody that is connected to their culture, to their tradition, but still represents the male and female within themselves." And she goes, "Yeah, I know what you're talking about." Then we started swapping stories about the two-spirit people on the reservation and talking about their roles within the

community. Some of them are spiritual roles. I don't claim myself to be one of those people, but I know, in terms of my family, what my place is. She then said, "You know what, I'm very happy for you because I think you came back; you came back into who you were supposed to be."

I think it's really interesting, as Native people, how we come out multiple times. We're coming back into recognizing who we are. And I think about that story a lot, because all this trouble that I've dragged myself through—to solidify my identity or to incorporate my identity, or to find it—I mean, it was always there. So I dragged myself through all of that, only to come out in the end knowing that there were people there that already knew and had sort of reserved a place for me to stand back into.

A lot of our emergence story talks about the two-spirit people. A lot of our ceremonies and a lot of our cultural dances still talk about the two-spirit people. If you look across a lot of different cultures, there's a lot of that representation of male and female embodied in one person. And there's some deities that are named after them. So when I hear Native American communities say, "Oh, well, that doesn't exist," my response to them is: "That's Western colonization talking. When you go back to your own tradition, and when you go back to those people who remember, they will tell you that we've always been here."

A lot of the political rhetoric that I hear, especially in the LGBTQI community, uses Stonewall as a benchmark. But our benchmark is our people, our communities, and those elders who remember and have stories told to them over and over and over again, that we exist.

A decade after recording this interview, I still think about it often. I was struck at the time, and even more so now, by Crisosto's generosity, patience, and commitment to teaching me and others who would later engage with their

story. I was a country-bumpkin white kid with zero experience working and establishing trust with Native people, and who had barely any experience in interviewing or recording oral histories. Given my greater (though still novice) understanding now of the ways in which the fields of anthropology and folklore, to which oral history is inherently connected, have been utilized, and often complicit in the process of colonization, I'm even more humbled and grateful that Crisosto invited me into their home and agreed to this interview.

At the end of interviews, I always ask people, "What would you want to know from other rural queer people that I didn't ask you, and is there anything you'd like to talk about that we didn't cover?" Crisosto took that opportunity to talk about some of the sensitivity documentarians need to practice when interviewing Indigenous people, and I remember leaving that interview with a lot of questions about my role in this work. It wasn't the first time I'd wondered about these themes, but the experience of spending an afternoon with Crisosto continued to shape my approach to this work. Who should tell what stories? What relationship should documentarians, journalists, and oral historians have to the communities we work with? Is shared queerness and rural upbringing enough to justify my documentation of rural queer experiences that are greatly different than my own, particularly across lines of race and class? And if so, how do we do this work justly, ethically, in ways that counter long histories of extraction and colonial power systems that have partially operated through the theft of Indigenous stories and culture?

The Two Spirit National Cultural Exchange is no longer in operation. Crisosto is now an English professor, and at the time of this writing, they have published two poetry collections: ~~GENESIS~~ (Lost Alphabet, 2018) and Ghostword (Gnashing Teeth, 2022). You can hear more of Crisosto's interview in season 1 of the Country Queers podcast, and you can find out more about their work and purchase their books at https://crisostoapache.com.

Wil Garten (left) and Loring Wagner (right) at their kitchen table, Edmond, Oklahoma, July 2014

WIL GARTEN he/him, 46 years old
LORING WAGNER he/him, 45 years old

Gáuigú (Kiowa), Wahzhazhe (Osage), Kitikiti'sh (Wichita), Nʉmʉnʉʉ
(Comanche), and Kiikaapoi (Kickapoo) lands
Edmond, Oklahoma
July 3, 2014

After seeing the project's Kickstarter campaign, Loring reached out and invited me to come visit him and his husband, Wil, in Edmond, Oklahoma. Their house, which they shared with a tiny dog named Sweetie, was full of cute quilts, country-themed cookie jars, and cool vintage lamps. Throughout the interview at their kitchen table, they interrupted each other in the sweetest way, and I remember laughing often. This interview was transcribed by e.m.i. broomfield.

WIL: As I was hitting my teenage years, I realized that I really didn't have anyone to talk to about being gay. Then, all of a sudden, you start seeing reports of AIDS and how it's impacting the homosexual community—

LORING: And we had no one to turn to—

WIL: No. There was no one to ask questions about it, for fear of them finding out that you're gay. And even when you got out into the gay community, it was a taboo topic, big time. It still is, to a certain degree. Nobody discusses it at the bars. And that's what the community in Oklahoma consists of, for

the most part. There are finally charitable organizations that are starting to get some news attention, but there's no other gathering places for gay people to meet outside of the bar. And, as we came out, a lot of our peers that were coming out with us were contracting AIDS. And a lot of them—

LORING: —suicide.

WIL: Yeah. A lot of them would commit suicide. Several of them went down so fast, it was just unbelievable.

LORING: Right in front of your eyes, and there was nothing you could do to help.

WIL: You'd see them one week, and they initially looked all healthy. Within a matter of months, you're going, *What the hell?* And at the bars— "Oh, did you hear that so-and-so died?"

"Yeah, they had AIDS." But you never really wanted to discuss it, so—

LORING: And you had slept with him!

WIL: Yeah, and you had no resources available to give you an education on what you could do to prevent it. They finally started coming out with, "Oh, well, use condoms!" Then all of a sudden you see these huge bowls of condoms popping up at the bars.

LORING: Punch bowls with condoms! What really sucked was that we were out at the bar and sexually active before we found out anything about how to not contract it. Because in the beginning they said, "Well, it's a virus, like a cold."

WIL: So you don't ascertain that necessarily as being contractible with sex.

LORING: And I'm like, "Oh, I kissed . . . how many guys last night?" Because back then, especially when you met, you kissed! It was just our typical greeting. You might even get dipped in the tongue! It was just very, very common, and not thought that much of. So it was like, "Okay, it's a done deal! We're all going, so why worry about it? Why even consider safe sex?" Especially because I'm allergic to latex. So it's like, "Forget safe sex. I've already been exposed to it God only knows how many thousands of times," so what was the point? You already had it.

WIL: So you partied wild, lived loose, and never planned for a future.

LORING: Ever. You had $1,000? Well your

wardrobe was getting one hell of a bumped-up look!

WIL: Get your rent caught up and update your wardrobe!

LORING: And coke for all your friends! Why not do the drugs, like I said earlier? There was no incentive not to. If it made the moment that much more fun, well, your buddy who was twenty-six and had just died would've encouraged you to do it. There were a lot of times you'd go out for a fun time, and instead you were basically at a wake. Tears and cheers, you know? To the person you lost—or not "person," the "people" you lost that week.

WIL: Yep. There were some weeks there were multiple people at a time.

LORING: And we weren't allowed to go to the funerals.

WIL: Yeah, a lot of the funerals, the parents didn't want their children to be gay to begin with, so when they did finally pass, they wouldn't allow gay people to show up at the funeral.

LORING: Westboro Baptist Church could go to

their funeral and protest, but we couldn't. It's the truth. The cops would get rid of us. They would escort us away from a funeral.

WIL: I was with somebody, Michael, for seven years who eventually succumbed to HIV and AIDS, and his only strife in life, the whole time that I had known him, was that he wanted his family to give him some acceptance. We were together five years before they ever allowed him to come home for Christmas. So the first time he went into the hospital with major health issues, I wasn't gonna call them. Michael finally came around, and he called his stepmom, Charlene, and she showed up with his youngest, nine-year-old sister. Well, Michael spent forty-five days in the hospital the first time, and the medications that he had to take on a daily basis were just toxic. Turned out he had a fungal infection in his spinal column, and he just refused to take them. It didn't matter if I shoved them down his throat or what. The second time he went into the hospital for a long period, his dad showed up, and I was informed by the stepmonster that I wasn't allowed to speak to the father. His father actually came out in the hallway and met me at the vending machine and tried to carry on a conversation, and of course I dismissed him. I had no respect for his family

whatsoever. I had no use for them.

Within three years of him being diagnosed, he was begging to move home. It was probably about two months before Michael passed away, he woke up one morning, and he said, "Well, I wanna move home." I was like, "Will your family let you?" And he was like, "Yeah!" I was like, "Well, if that's what you wanna do, let's do it." So we were packing up the apartment, and he was going, "Well, can I take this? Can I take that?" It was like, "Michael, we've got seven years here. If there's something in this house you want, take it." Which was the whole house! We had new furniture, we had big-screen TVs. I was like, "If it's gonna make him happy, let's do it." His parents lived just outside of Shreveport—so we get down there, and his stepmom is like, "Where are you gonna live?" I'm like, "Michael, I thought you said that you could live there?" And he's like, "My dad did." And I was like, "Well, then get your dad on the phone." And he was like, "He's not talking to me now."

So his stepmom's like, "I'll meet you in the hotel." This was after we had already driven all night, and we had been up the previous day loading the U-Haul truck. It's the Friday before Memorial Day. No places are open to check out rentals or anything. So finally I was like, "You know what, let's just offload it into a storage unit." And he's like, "We can't afford that." And I'm like, "We can afford that, it's no big deal." So we offload into the storage unit, and Charlene finally agreed to let him come stay for the week, and said they would do something about finding a place. They found him an apartment in this *god-awful* neighborhood.

I talked with him daily. He found out I was coming back down to visit. It was July Fourth weekend, and when I got down there, he had spent every ounce of energy he had just to try and get the apartment unpacked, and pictures on the walls, and all of that stuff. I walk in the door, and there are roaches everywhere. The kitchen is just covered with them. And he's like, "I told them I was having problems with them," and I was like, "Michael, this isn't 'problems,' this is infestation!" He's like, "I know." I was like, "Have they done anything?" And he's like, "Well, they brought this down." And at this point, he had lost so much weight that he was weak. They had a five-gallon bucket of roach spray that they had left for him to spray the apartment with that he couldn't even lift.

That night I sprayed down his house. Every stitch of clothing in his bedroom was completely dirty. I was like, "Isn't your stepmom coming over and helping you do laundry?" And he was like, "No, she hasn't been here since my dad moved me in." And I was like, "Really?! Your sisters? Your brother?"

"No." So the next day, I get up, get all of his clothes piled up, we meander over to the laundry room. It took us twenty minutes to get over there, which was only fifty feet away, but he was insistent he wanted to come. We did eight loads of laundry, and then he dozed off. When he woke up, I said, "We need to go to Walmart, because this shit that they gave you for roaches isn't going to suffice. I need to buy some powerful chemicals."

At this point, he literally looked like a sixty-year-old man. His skin was gray. He was wore down completely, and I'm thinking, *I'm not so certain I should leave him here.* Throughout the rest of the weekend, I bombed the hell out of his apartment—put down roach traps, got some Roach Prufe. I went along all the baseboards. By the next morning, you couldn't find a live roach in that place.

LORING: That was back when they had chemicals that worked!

WIL: So, my time was running out. You know? It was rolling up on Sunday afternoon, and I was like, "Okay, well, I need to go. I gotta be at work in the morning. Why don't you just hop in the truck with me and come home?" He's like, "No, I'm good here. I've got a doctor's appointment tomorrow," and I was like, "Okay. Who's taking you?" and he says, "My mom is gonna come over."

So, Charlene apparently did show up to take him to the doctor's appointment that Monday. Once they were at the doctor's, they immediately sent him to the emergency room, and they admitted him into the hospital. Michael called me from the hospital and said, "Oh, I'm doing a lot better. They're gonna get me all fixed up!" And so we talked every day.

That Wednesday, I'd woken him up and spoken with him, and I felt a little guilty. So that Thursday I didn't call him, because I didn't want to wake him up, just in case he was resting. I talked to him Friday, and then Saturday morning his stepmom was on the phone to tell me he had passed away at six o'clock in the morning. I was like, "You guys didn't call me to let me know he was that bad?"

"Oh, well, we didn't have time. We needed to get the preacher in here."

The funeral was held the following Monday, so I had a day to get down there. I called my job to let them know I would not be in on Monday, and my boss at that time—who I thought was a really good friend—the first thing she said when I told her I needed to go for Michael's funeral was, "Oh, well, you know that I can't pay you bereavement pay?"

And I'm like, "I still have vacation."

"Yeah, but typically you need to give notice for that."

I was like, "Are you going to allow me to use vacation? Or I can do it without pay, whatever, it's your choice."

"Oh no, you take as much time as you need."

"So basically what you're saying is, I need to be back at work on Tuesday?"

"That would be nice."

LORING: That's how we were all treated.

WIL: Yeah. And Michael's brother Cliff called me to find out what I wanted from the apartment. He was like, "Well, Dad and I are over here cleaning out his apartment." I was like, "Cliff, it's Saturday afternoon. He just passed away this morning."

"Yeah, Dad thought it'd be a good thing."

"What?!" I said, "You can't sit here and give me five minutes to get what I want out of the apartment? I bought all that shit! It's all mine."

"Well, we're gonna clean it out, and put it in your storage, so if there's anything special that you want to keep . . ."

My mother and aunt showed up shortly after I got the phone call that he'd passed, and Mom is like, "I'll go down with you." So we go down to Shreveport. We get down there Sunday night, get up Monday morning, go to the funeral. The stepmother wouldn't even look at me. The rest of the family wasn't even there. Michael's dad apparently was so distraught over losing him that he was just sitting in a pew in the family section, not speaking to anybody. Cliff wasn't allowed to come over and talk to me, but he sent a message that he wanted to see me after the funeral. I was like, "Okay." As the funeral begins to proceed, I was the only male that was in the visitor's section of the entire church—

LORING: It's 'cause he was gay.

WIL: Yeah. However, I do have to admit, there were a lot of ladies there—which was a fascinating thing to me. They filled up the church. Michael's oldest brother was sitting at the back of the family section in handcuffs, with the sheriff's deputy, 'cause he was still in prison.

So, we get halfway through the funeral, and this preacher is going on and on about needing to be saved, and all of this stuff. I'm like, "This is fuckin' bullshit." So I start to stand up. Of course, my mother yanks me down. I'm like, "What are you doing!"

She's like, "You can't do this. This isn't about you!"

I was like, "Bitch, it *is* about me! She finally convinced me.

So we get through the funeral. It's time to get up and walk out, and I'm not even gonna pay respects to the family. I had no respect for them. But again, my mother turns me in their direction and walks us through the family. And of course, Charlene is the first one. She totally tries to dismiss me before Cliff elbows her, and then she kinda leans in and gives me this fake hug. So I just grabbed ahold of her and said, "Charlene, one of these days, when you least expect it—you're not gonna know when, you're not gonna know where—I am going to find you, and I am going to kill your ass. You are an evil cunt." And she just kind of stepped back a little bit, eyes wide as could be. I was like, "So good to see you."

LORING: She probably didn't know a Yankee knew how to act proper at a southern funeral!

WIL: Michael's dad was next. There were thirty people who had been in front of me, paying respects to the family, and Michael's dad did not get up for one person. All of a sudden, this man stands up, buttons his jacket, shakes my hand, pulls me into him, and says, "I want you to know something." He goes, "I want to thank you."

"For what?"

He goes, "When I was cleaning out Michael's pictures"—Michael took all of the pictures—he goes, "I can't ever remember seeing my son smile like that." He goes, "You validated that he was happy, and I want to thank you for that." I was like, "Well, you should have done it a lot sooner." He goes, "I know." I was like, "Well, I appreciate it." He goes, "Well, you don't know how much I appreciate what you've done." And he hugged my mother, and thanked her for making Michael a part of the family, and letting him be around, and then he unbuttoned his coat, sat back down, and didn't talk to anyone else.

LORING: Back then, you had to pull your boots up fast.

WIL: Yeah, I got to work the next day. They're all trying to play the sympathy card. I was like, "No. Y'all need to go away. I have a job to do. I ain't got time for this shit." I think they realized at that point I was pissed.

RAE: It's . . . *crazy.*

LORING: Yeah, my mom and family still are like, "You sure aren't much for going to funerals." But it's like, why would I be when we weren't allowed to go to most of our friends'?

WIL: We'd just pick a night, and all get together at the club and have drinks and talk about our friend and the years past.

LORING: Nobody tried to attend the services anymore; too many people had been turned away. And now, to this day, I have a real issue going to a funeral.

This excerpt brings up so many emotions and thoughts that it's hard to distill them. I knew the AIDS epidemic was a horrifying, terrifying era for LGBTQIA2S+ communities. I knew people died slow, painful, confusing deaths and experienced intense hatred and lack of care along the way. But this was the first time in my life that I heard stories of the AIDS epidemic directly from people who had survived it. It was the first time I heard stories of the AIDS epidemic outside of major coastal cities. And it was the first time I conducted an

interview that dove so deeply into the depths of trauma.

Sitting across the table from Wil and Loring, listening, decades after Michael had passed, to every minute detail of that last week of his life—still plain as day in Wil's mind—knocked the breath out of me. After they went outside to smoke, I took deep breaths in an effort to ward off the tears beginning to fill my eyes. I felt completely unqualified, undeserving of receiving such an offering of vulnerability, honesty, and embodied small-town queer history. Afterward, late at night at a Denny's, I laughed till I cried at Wil and Loring's commentary, under their breath, about the diners all around us.

Wil passed away in 2021 from cancer. I wrote to Loring in October 2023 asking for his approval to include this excerpt and inviting him to share any memories or reflections. This is an excerpt of his reply:

Hello Rae! I'm sorry that it's taken me so long to get to this. I knew I would cry but wasn't sure how I would get through this. I'm glad to say, there's been happy tears with the sad.

Wil passed away on June 3, 2021. He was fifty-two, and it'd been thirty years of dealing with HIV. He died of cancer. Amazingly, he passed peacefully and pain free, at home in my arms. We had been talking and making our peace. He was smiling. Our little dog Sweetie is now in heaven with Wil.

I have observed the old Southern tradition of a three-year mourning. I'm going to be okay. I believe the story should be told. There is validity in this, and this is the history of our people. Love you! And thank you! You're shouldering the burden of writing a small part of our history. This will be around when we are long gone. 🖤🩶

Crystal Middlestadt at Villanueva State Park, New Mexico, July 2014

CRYSTAL MIDDLESTADT they/them, 34 years old

Pueblos, Núuchi-u (Ute), Jicarilla Apache, and Ndé Kónitsą̃ą́íí Gokíyaa (Lipan Apache) lands
Ribera, New Mexico
July 7, 2014

As the route began to take shape, I emailed everyone I knew along the way, asking if they knew any country queers. My friend Riley in Denver put me in touch with Crystal. At the time of this interview, Crystal was living in Villanueva, New Mexico, and working at the post office in the nearby town of Ribera. This interview was recorded at a picnic table in Villanueva State Park, just a short walk down the road from the house where Crystal lived at the time. I stayed the night on Crystal's couch and had dinner with them, their roommate, their roommate's kiddo, and their lesbian neighbors. This interview was transcribed by Jocelyn Jessop.

CRYSTAL: I grew up in Oregon and then lived in Denver for ten years. About five years ago, people in my friend group were all aware of climate change and how the economy is never going to be the same, and lots of things that made us think differently about what choices we're going to make in the future, where we'd want to live, and geographically what places feel secure—not so much in terms of war or whatnot, but in terms of access to resources, access to shelter, access to water. So I'd been having those conversations with friends about survivalist things. Not like "We're gonna join a far-right-preppers group in Idaho," but "Where are the fruit trees in town?" and "Who has what skills?" Then my friend, who I live with now—she'd been coming down here to New Mexico as part of a spiritual community for several years. I started to visit with her and planted the intention of helping raise her child down here, which she did not want to do in the city.

I was on my own spiritual path. I was starting to make different decisions in my life based on what was feeling right and trying to follow those intuitions. I was co–executive director of a statewide queer antiviolence organization for six years. It was exciting work, but it was really intense too: working on murder cases, training victim advocates, and organizing youth. I knew that for the organization's health and for my own health, I didn't want to stay there much longer.

And, on a deeper level, I wanted to have the experience of being in a community where there was more interdependency because when you're in a small town, you need each other more tangibly than you do in a city. I wanted to live out some of those values that were such a big part of my politics, and I was getting tired of how in cities people can just up and go. They can up and go to a different organization if there's a personality conflict, they can move to a different city, they can hop around to different places and not really have to do the work or really invest in people in that way. I was ready for that kind of challenge. I also wanted to be away from everything. I was looking forward to the solitude. I love being outdoors. I love going on road trips. I love camping. So it seemed great to live somewhere where I could literally walk to the state park every day. I had a lot of romanticized feelings about it all.

RAE: Do you feel like that job, focused on violence, gave you any ideas of rural places being unsafe for queer people?

CRYSTAL: No, because I saw so much violence in Denver as well, and in other urban areas around the country; because I also served on the governance committee for the National Coalition of Anti-Violence Programs. When you're actually in that work all the time and you don't just see what the media puts out, you see that it really does happen everywhere. It can be just as brutal on your block in downtown wherever as it can on a country road. Being out here, I feel super safe. I haven't had one experience yet that feels like mistreatment, or even a microaggression.

Before I started doing antiviolence-specific work, I was teaching self-defense. It was verbal, physical, and mental, and so we talked a lot about being socialized into the victim role, about boundary-setting and verbal skills, but also just learning to trust yourself. So I've just been immersed in this world of safety, on an individual and a community level. Then I went in to doing queer-specific work, which included hate violence, police brutality, sexual assault, domestic violence. I got comfortable and used to moving through life being prepared for the worst-case scenario, where I'd be thinking about what targets I could hit if I had to. Or, if I'm at a club and someone's disrespecting my friend, I will not hesitate to get between them, because I know what to do if it escalates. I just had a certain level of hardness with people that I didn't even realize was normal to me.

Out here, you can't be like that, 'cause then you're just rude, you know? Or you're really unfriendly. And you don't want to treat people like that. Here, I'm just learning a different way of being. I'm learning to walk down my street or go into the store, and to expect to be treated like anyone else that might walk in there. And I'm continually having that experience, so it's getting affirmed every day. That feels really good.

It's a relief, but I also think it just feels like a healthier way to live my life—to keep my heart more open to people in general and to be authentic about it, instead of always bracing for potential harm, whether that's emotional or physical, and then missing opportunities to connect with someone on a human level. This is giving me a chance to practice that way of being present with the world around me. I think people in cities— we should practice more of that.

I think often of this concluding moment from my interview with Crystal. It was so refreshing, and surprising, to hear a radical leftist queer person with deep connections to major cities talk about the lessons they were learning about authenticity, presence, and kindness from country people. So often the narratives about rural people, including in national leftist spaces, position them as overwhelmingly conservative, closed minded, and hateful. I was moved by Crystal's reflections on what they were learning from rural people. Also resonant was Crystal's description of the conversations they were having with friends in Denver about how to survive and take care of each other in the uncertain days ahead on this planet.

Twig and his dog Sasquatch on their porch in Pecos, New Mexico, July 2014

TWIG DELUJÉ he/him, 31 years old

Pueblos, Núuchi-u (Ute), and Ndé Kónitsąą́íí Gokíyaa (Lipan Apache) lands
Pecos, New Mexico
July 8, 2014

I got connected to Twig when his then girlfriend wrote me an email telling me I should interview him, and then put us in touch. The morning after I had spent a full day and night at Crystal's house in Ribera, I drove up to Twig's green single-wide trailer on a wooded hillside outside Pecos. I was late because I'd run into issues backing up audio and photo files that morning, finding myself in a frenzy worrying that files had been lost. Despite my running late, Twig welcomed me with coffee and a big, delicious homemade breakfast. His gigantic dogs, Sasquatch and Alo, slept nearby throughout our conversation. This interview was transcribed by Kayden Moore.

TWIG: My mom had two really good friends when I was growing up, and one of them was a trans lady. I was just talking to one of my friends about this a couple weeks ago; how I knew as a kid that you could transition from masculine to feminine, but not the other way around. I was always kind of . . . I want to say butch, but more like masculine presenting. Not even tomboy-ish; I liked things that "guys" liked. So I was just going along the lines of being a butch woman. Then

I went to college and got a lot more exposure to differences in gender. Because also, growing up in Kansas, there *is* something to a stereotypical Midwestern softball lesbian! And I was like, "That is so not me. I hate sports. I have nothing to do with softball. I don't watch games." So I joked for a long time with one of my good friends that I was going to turn into a trucker dyke, like, a diesel dyke. And they were like, "Please don't do that!" And I was like, "Why? It's not about you." You know? Lo and behold, that's exactly what happened, only I grew a beard!

But thinking about being male or masculine presenting, and growing up not being able to call it what it was: I remember, every time I played make believe as a kid, I would be somebody else. Every frickin' time, I was *always* a blonde boy named Jack—because I was super blonde when I was a kid. Every single time. I was just trying to be somebody I wanted to be, and I didn't have any names for it. So yeah, after I finally was able to get on testosterone, I realized that I was actually overcompensating for a lot before I had a name or knew exactly what was going on for me. So pre-T, or pre–trans identified, I was walking around presenting as uber, uber masculine, trying to make my voice lower, trying to take up a lot more space in a way I perceived as being masculine.

Then, once my hormones got figured out, once my brain started to kind of relax— because I was actually seeing what I wanted to see in the mirror—then I got uber swishy. So now, before people hear me talk, they are like, "Who the fuck is that?" and get really nervous 'cause I look butch and redneck-y at times. But then I talk, and it all goes away. So I just needed to find that balance. Now I feel way better 'cause I feel like I get to sit in the middle, and that feels really good to me.

I identify as a country queer, and it took me a long time to get here—as I'm sure it does for many people—of melding, or finding the balance or marriage between those two things. Because we're not always taught, or told, that they can coexist. But they can. That varies in how that works and what that looks like from person to person, but for me it was finding that comfort again in myself, knowing that I like being in the country, I like throwing hatchets, and being out in the woods. I like doing things that don't involve a lot of other people. I grasp so hard onto my identity as a rural queer that trying to think of myself as anything else at this point in my life is almost unfathomable.

I don't want to hurt anybody's feelings, but I feel like people in cities, for a large part, get very wrapped up in a lot of politics. Not just governmental politics, but also gender politics. But I feel like, when you're in a rural existence, sometimes you're more concerned about your garden or your next meal, or the safety of your pets or your livestock. And again, I'm just speaking from my own experience, but I find that, when I'm living out in a rural area, I'm less concerned about what other queers think of my queerness or my existence than when I'm in a big city.

I get a lot of flak from people for the kind of family I want, 'cause I don't actually want children. I don't want to get married. I can totally see myself with a partner, but I also don't feel like that's required. I get feedback sometimes that makes me feel like it's a cold place to come from, like there's something wrong with me for not wanting to have that whole biological-family thing. But my ideal family looks like a slew of dogs and some cats on five acres with a big, huge garden, and a beefalo named Tawanda. That's what I want! I'm a really, really independent individual, and I think that's hard for a lot of people to wrap their minds around. Because a lot of people do get a lot from queer community, especially in a rural place, because it's so difficult to find. But yeah, I'm not a fan of kids. I love baby goats. I love baby animals. People argue with me all the time that human children are baby animals, and I say, "Nope! Not the same. At all."

I had so much fun talking with Twig and meeting his dogs (both of them have since passed on). We talked about writing, about our sheroes (including Dorothy Allison, whose interview lies farther ahead in this book). There's so much of Twig's vision of a future family that resonates with me. As I write this, I take breaks to look out the window at my goats grazing among the late-fall goldenrod. *I hear the ducks fussing at me to feed them, and feel my dogs' eyes on my back, wondering when, when, when we'll take our evening walk. It isn't necessarily everything I've ever dreamed of for a family of my own, but it is a wonderful and sweet cross-species crew to do life with on this hillside. I love knowing there are other country queers out there making intraspecies family and finding deep comfort and connection within it.*

Cameron (left) and Jon (right) at home with the horses, Avondale, Colorado, July 2014

CAMERON McCOY he/him, 45 years old

Tsitsistas (Cheyenne), Núuchi-u (Ute), Ndé Kónitsą̄ą́íí Gokíyaa
(Lipan Apache), and Jicarilla Apache lands
Avondale, Colorado
July 9, 2014

After seeing the project's Kickstarter, Cameron invited me out to the horse rescue ranch he runs with his husband, Jon Peck. When I sit down with couples, usually one person is into the interview and the other is somewhat bored and skeptical. I remember Jon mostly just wanting to talk about the horses. After our interview, they walked around the property while I made photos of them interacting with a large gaggle of horses and dogs. Cameron, with his years of experience on the road as a trucker, sent me on my way with a recommendation for an affordable but nice hotel nearby. This interview was transcribed by e.m.i. broomfield.

CAMERON: I used to drive a truck. My grandparents owned a machine shop out in a rural area in Kansas, so during high school I would go out there and spend the summers with them. I went out and did farming stuff and drove trucks on the weekends. After high school, there was a guy who wanted me to drive for him in the winter, when there was no farmwork. He had a trucking company that hauled grain, but he was starting a tanker-trucking company hauling milk. So I started the milk division up for him. I had

about twenty trucks on my side. I lived about 120 miles from him, in a different location. I didn't hide being gay from him, but I didn't broadcast it. There was a girl there at the company that—growing up, when I thought I was straight—would've been my perfect wife. She was a little blonde thing, real pretty, had a degree from Kansas State in agronomics. She was basically everything I pictured my wife would be someday. She always flirted with me, and I just never flirted back. Then one day, in front of the whole office, she was like, "It's cold outside, you need to come over tonight and keep me warm." I just ignored her.

The next day, the boss called me in, and he goes, "Well, I wanna know something. I wanna know if you're gay. My sister is a lesbian, and I don't have a problem with it, but I wanted to know." I told him I am. The next day he called me in again and he said, "There's too much testosterone in the trucking industry. We can't have gays workin' for us."

So, what do you do? There's not any laws to protect you out there. To make things worse, it was a real small town, where my dad was the sheriff and my mom was a kindergarten teacher. And I didn't live there—I was just in and out all the time for work. So, I could have started a bunch of shit, but it wasn't my town, and I didn't want to make things difficult for my parents. It was better that I just leave.

That's when I decided I'd go ahead and get my own truck. I went to work for a company in Wichita. Started out as a dispatcher. Then I became their operations manager. The owners were close to retirement age, so their daughter was running it, and she was about my age. There were a lot of things that sucked about that company, but they had no problems with gay. So many of the people there are like the people around here—if you get to know somebody before they figure out you're gay, and then they find out, it's not that big of a deal. Where, if I just went in as gay, it would have been a problem. I think I changed a lot of attitudes there. By the time I left, I had probably 120 employees under me in all our six different terminals. I ran the whole thing. And they all knew. And nothing hateful was tolerated—nothing racial, nothing gay.

One of my goals has always been to go to every state, and I've been to forty-seven now. My dog—not this dog; this is Junior— but the one that he's the junior of, was with me. So he played in both oceans, and everything else. One time I was going from Kansas City to Minneapolis, which isn't a very long trip, but I had, like, five days to do it. So I went to Omaha on a Thursday night, and it sucked. Then I went to Des Moines on

a Friday night and met Jon there at the bar. The next night, I saw him again, and then I went on up to Minneapolis, and . . . within a few weeks, I sold my semi and moved to Iowa to be with Jon.

This is one of my favorite love stories I've heard in over a decade of interviewing country queers. I also really appreciate what Cameron shared about why he decided not to raise a big fuss after being fired for being gay. This story taps into some of the complicated navigations many of us wade through as country queers, especially those of us still living close to our families of origin and/or in the towns and counties where we were raised. From the outside, this kind of approach may seem apolitical or passive. But I've made similar choices in my life not to make a fuss about homophobic or transphobic dynamics in a workplace. The reality is that in small-town and country life, you often don't have the choice of isolating yourself from a broader community with whom you may disagree politically or religiously. Even across difference, rural people often depend on each other to survive, taking care of each other.

THE OVERWHELM

2015–2019

Within a month of returning home from the epic 2014 summer road trip, I was back at work in rural West Virginia public schools. I quickly became aware that I couldn't build an online project aimed at increasing rural queer visibility while working at a job where I couldn't even be out at work (though all the queer kids found me and came out to me anyway). I had a computer folder chock-full of almost forty interviews, no time to transcribe them, and new questions about how to best share them in an easily accessible but also engaging way. I wanted to learn more about oral history and multimedia storytelling, and I had quickly developed a whole lot of questions about the complicated issues of power inherent in documentary work around race, class, gender, and insider/outsider dynamics. I felt completely overwhelmed, but also hooked on this project and this work. I wanted to keep doing it, but I knew I needed to learn more, to find time for more intentional study, to find mentors and teachers who could help me make sense of what I had gathered and what might happen next.

I ended up applying, and was accepted, to a master's program in folklore at the University of North Carolina at Chapel Hill—home to the Southern Oral History Program and a brilliant staff of American studies and folklore professors, and through which I could take classes at Duke University's Center for Documentary Studies. Naively, I thought a two-year master's program would give me time and space to truly focus on the project. As it turns out, this is not how MA programs work. In many ways it wasn't the best fit, and I gained *significant* additional student loan debt. But I made some great connections while there, and I got to work with my now friend and one of the editorial advisors of the *Country Queers* podcast, Dr. Sharon P. Holland.

I began the program in August 2015, and while in grad school I lived on a queer farm outside of town and experimented in semi-collective rural queer life. I was achingly homesick for the mountains, but after four years living back home in West Virginia, I was curious to try out rural queer life only a thirty-minute drive from a very queer, trans, and political city like Durham.

After grad school, I got hired as the public affairs director at WMMT 88.7 FM, a nonprofit community radio station based at Appalshop, a celebrated media, arts, and education center in the coalfields of eastern Kentucky. I was responsible for eight hours a week of radio content; some I produced myself, some I supported community producers in making, and some I downloaded from the Public Radio Exchange. I also worked part time as a volunteer contributing editor for *Scalawag* magazine for several years, prioritizing stories from and about the rural South. During those years, weekly "takeovers" on the Country Queers Instagram account were the main content the project helped elevate. They were a lot of fun at first, but attempting to manage and moderate a community space on a social media platform is tricky, incredibly time consuming, and ultimately not something I wanted to continue. Working a full-time radio job, editing for the then new magazine, and simultaneously coordinating the Instagram takeovers left me worn out.

During this period, I had very little time or energy to dedicate to the project. There was no funding coming in, and my chronic illness got drastically worse, at times making it difficult for me to work. Big questions emerged about financial and energetic sustainability, how to best make these stories accessible to other rural LGBTQIA2S+ people, and my role as a white person

leading a project of this scope and scale. I became much more intentional about who I interviewed and why, particularly prioritizing interviews with Black country queers and trans folks after learning in the earlier years that those most likely to self-select for the project were cisgender and white narrators. I also recorded far fewer interviews during this time than in the first two years, realizing that my initial approach of interviewing anyone who would talk to me had quickly landed me with a heaping plate of overwhelm. I weighed the pros and cons of trying to continue with the original dream of a book versus pivoting to a podcast. I swam through confusion about all the ideas other people had contributed for what Country Queers could or should become: a web series, an interactive map, a documentary film, a series of YouTube videos, a zine, a mobile recording studio, a crowdsourced story center.

In 2019, a small community arts gallery in Athens, Ohio, reached out asking if I'd ever considered putting together a gallery exhibit, so I applied for Country Queers' first-ever grant: $3,000 from the Kentucky Foundation for Women to bring the show to life. My dad helped me print and mat the photographs, using frames we'd bought at Goodwill that he spray-painted, glitterified, and bedazzled at my request. That opening was delightful, and people expressed gratitude for the images and stories displayed within. Despite my having a full-time job with benefits (for the first time since starting the project), between my lemon of a used Subaru constantly requiring expensive repairs (even as I was still paying off the loan) and a consistent and hard to quell flare-up of my ulcerative colitis (and with this the added costs and time drain of frequent doctor appointments, lab work, and medications), there was no clear way to take the exhibit to more places after that first exhibition closed.

This quieter, slower, and less certain chapter of the project was full of doubt, overwhelm, confusion, and exhaustion for me. I spent a lot of this time feeling paralyzed about what direction to take the project in, and frankly, feeling unconvinced it would ever become anything more than Instagram takeovers and a pile of untranscribed interviews gathering proverbial dust on my hard drive. I worried that in this era of clickbait, memes, and thirst traps driving algorithms and money flow on social media, there wasn't a desire in the world for complex, nuanced, slow, rural queer oral histories.

In retrospect, I'm glad the project didn't emerge into the world in podcast or book form during this era. This work wasn't ready yet, and I wasn't either.

Sharon P. Holland at home outside Chapel Hill, North Carolina, June 2017

SHARON P. HOLLAND she/her, 54 years old

Occaneechi, Eno, and Haliwa-Saponi lands
Chapel Hill, North Carolina
June 5, 2017

Sharon teaches in the Department of American Studies of the University of North Carolina at Chapel Hill—a fact that in part inspired me to enroll in the folklore master's program housed there. I took a theory class with her that made my brain stretch in ways it never had before. My partner at the time was chosen family with Sharon, so I spent many evenings eating her incredible cooking in her gorgeous home. Following my graduation, just before leaving North Carolina, I interviewed Sharon in her home office in the woods outside Chapel Hill. In addition to being on my thesis committee, she was at the top of my list of advisors for the Country Queers *podcast. I'm so grateful she said yes. Over the years, Sharon has helped this project and my thinking become sharper and clearer in countless ways. I'm proud to call her a friend and mentor.*

SHARON: When I first bought the land, I was excited because I was like, "I want to live in a place with acreage, and I want to live in a place with a driveway, and with an old shed on it that looks kind of country and kind of scary at the same time." I wanted to live at the end of a dirt road, and this is, like, the end of the dirt road for Blackness, in that it's ten minutes from town, just in case anything breaks off. You can be a country queer all you want, but you also need to be safe. Or to find spaces of safety.

My people have been from this area. I'm probably a sixth-generation North Carolinian. I take it seriously, and I never really had a home. My mom and I moved around a lot. I grew up somewhere between a military brat and something else, and if I was going to put down roots, I wanted to put down roots where I could stay, and not be afraid of, like, "Oh, God, what's going on down the road?" So, there's a vibe here. There's these families, Black families, that have been here for generations. It's a mostly African American road, which is very unusual for Orange County.

I wanted to give a name to the property, and I thought of it as very sweet. A lot of people think it's kind of like a sanctuary. It was my non-bio brother, Eton, who was visiting once, and he said, "Why don't you call it Sweet Negritude?" And I'm like, "Yeah! Because Blackness is bittersweet." And because it seemed to resonate with the intellectual thought that brought me to all the things in my life that I think are good.

RAE: Do you want to say more about that?

SHARON: The Negritude movement. Pan-Africanism. I always tell people I'm African American culturally, I'm a person of African descent as a human—but then we all are—and I am Black politically, in that I believe in Black freedom and struggles for global Blackness. And I wouldn't know anything about those struggles if I hadn't read Frantz Fanon or Aimé Césaire, W. E. B. Du Bois, Harriet Tubman, or about Tubman at least. Harriet Jacobs. Just all those struggles for Black freedom, and very complicated struggles among complicated people. I guess that's what I like about the term "Negritude." It talks about Black freedom, Black genius, but it also talks about that we're more than just our suffering, and I think that's important. So, this place is about more than just Black suffering. It's about the gift of Blackness.

I guess the closest thing to my own self-identification would be two-spirit, without utilizing a term that I know has been churned around in LGBTQIA spaces, to some good effect and others not. I really do feel like I'm both male and female, of yin and yang, and I'm proud of both those qualities. And so, I will walk down the street in a tie and see a nice piece of mid-century modern furniture in the window and go, "Oh my God, that's a fabulous dresser!" Some would probably say I'm a gay man trapped inside

a lesbian's body. But I don't think of him as trapped; I think of him as very much at home. You know? I love feeding other people, I love all manner of queer creativity, and I like radical thought. So how do I identify? I try to be ethical. When I'm not, it weighs on me *forever*. I guess I'd say I am gendered and genderless at the same time. I don't really stick to its codes. And I love the aesthetic. I love art. I think that beauty is underrated and overarticulated, definitionally. I feel the people I love should grow up surrounded by beauty.

I guess there's a lot about how I live and who I am that a lot of folks don't understand, but if I could give a small window into that understanding, it's that most people's encounter of Blackness is through narratives that are historical registers, but they're not necessarily experientially or culturally marked. And so, I remember watching *Hidden Figures*, a movie—unfortunately I'm going to put this on tape—I really did not like. And part of it is: I'm sick of seeing us pull white attention to Blackness through Black suffering. There have got to be some other avenues, right? One of the things I loved about the film, though, is that if you were born into Black bourgeois middle-class culture, the aesthetic landscape of that culture was all mid-century modern.

So people will come into the house and they think I'm invested in the bastions of whiteness. But I'm like, "Well, actually, this is part of the culture I grew up with." Where someone would say, "Girl, you better use a coaster with my coffee table!" Or, like, the plastic on the furniture down South, right? There was plastic on it because, guess what? Those women knew it was art! And I think that's a beautiful thing! I guess what I'm trying to say is, I wish radical folks had a real sense that beauty is okay, and also a real sense of how each of us lives.

At the same time, when I moved to the South, one of my Black friends was like, "Oh, God, are you going to be okay down there?" I'm like, "They have running toilets. I think I'll be okay. And my people are from here. I got this."

When I broke up from my twelve-year relationship and decided that I'm finally going to live how I've always wanted to live, I bought this house at the end of the road on eight acres. I had people messaging me on Facebook and leaving me texts. "Girl, are you going to be okay? You're a *Black* woman." "Mmm, Sharon done moved out in the woods, girl. All *by* herself! Ain't nan person around. Okay?"

I remember my friend, Laura Bells, bless her heart. She worked over at Watts Grocery. When I left that long-term relationship and moved out here from Durham, she goes, "I'm coming out there to see you, and you know I can't drive at night." She's very high femme, hilarious, a good, good, good friend. She was like, "I can't drive at night, but I'm gonna come see you." And sure if she didn't drive her little Mustang up here. She goes, "Lord, girl, you got gravel in my heels!" She came up, and we did some porch sitting, 'cause she's from Randleman, North Carolina, so, you know, she like the country too. And it was just really sweet. She just wanted to know. She goes, "I ain't worried about the country. I just want to know you okay." But you know, people were a little worried.

So, the combination is a little bit weird. It's like, you could be living in a Chicago loft on the inside, but on the outside you're like, "I been clearing that land for a half a month now and I can't get that stump out. You gotta guy with a haul?" You know what I mean? The conversations I have with people seem so bifurcated, but not so much to me, because I grew up in that mid-century modern world. That aesthetic world of the beautiful black dress, the cocktail party, and the Eames furniture. Then there was my grandmother's farm that had been in her family for generations, that we were in the process of losing when I was a kid that I would go out to every once in a while.

I got this place because I wanted peace. I wanted to be as far away from the world as possible, while still being able to get ten minutes within good foodie culture. Sometimes for days, I don't see cars. You forget to care. You find yourself driving down the road and going, "This is not acceptable! I need to go back home and put on undergarments." Or you're walking on the land, and you put your high boots on because you think, "Oh, it's raining really hard. Let's go down to the creek and see how high."

It's just a state of mind, and it's peace. And I just want to tell people: rural space doesn't belong to the rednecks, whoever the fuck they are. I don't believe in that term. It doesn't belong to whiteness. It doesn't belong to anyone. I don't consider myself integrating. Maybe that's why I'm out here: because I don't have to desegregate it. And I feel my humanity in ways that I have to be mindful about.

How much land am I clearing? What am I getting rid of to put this up? Am I truly the caretaker of this place?

Sharon is one of those people whose brain is so magnificent that I often can't keep up, but I love to sit and listen to her talk. She thinks in ever-expanding circles, starting with some complex theoretical concept, threading it through a scene in a Toni Morrison novel, tying that to a story of working with her horse, Annie, bringing us back through accounts of the Middle Passage, and returning to a piece of writing by Hortense Spillers. Listening to her almost feels like watching ripples in water moving outward.

Having her on the podcast advisory team has been crucial. Her blunt, no-nonsense approach is also full of love and care. She always answers my angsty emails and texts about the project with a sense of humor and calm. After one particularly challenging summer of chronic illness flare-up, a dried-up spring for weeks, plus being extremely broke despite working four part-time jobs, I wrote the editorial advisory team an email saying, "I'm sick. I'm burnt out. I think Country Queers needs to end. I'll be in touch soon to talk more with you all about it." None of them replied, and a few weeks later when Sharon and I caught up on the phone, she teased me about it, saying they all just decided to let me calm down a bit first. She said to me, "You didn't choose this work, Rae. It chose you." You can hear more of Sharon's interview in season 1 of the podcast, and you can order her brilliant books online.

Robyn Thirkill at home with her goats, Prospect, Virginia, September 2016

ROBYN THIRKILL she/her, 41 years old

Monacan and Occaneechi lands
Prospect, Virginia
September 3, 2016

Robyn and I met on the dating app OkCupid sometime during the first two years of Country Queers' existence. We spent a few weeks writing occasional messages back and forth about our farm lives. I didn't have internet at home or a cell phone, so I'd log into OkCupid from my laptop at the public library in town. I was always super nervous that a student I worked with in the public schools, or one of their parents, would see me messaging queers on a dating app and out me at work. Robyn had goats, and I wanted some. She had beehives, and I did too. I had ducks, and I think she had chickens. We never went on a date or met up, but I asked her if she'd be up for doing an interview for Country Queers *sometime, and she said yes. A couple years later, when I was in graduate school in North Carolina, I drove up to Prospect, Virginia, and spent the afternoon talking with her in her living room. Her dog was next door in the other half of the duplex she shares with her mom. After the interview, we walked around her property so I could make pictures of her with the goats and dogs.*

ROBYN: Prospect is just outside of Farmville, Virginia, between Richmond and Lynchburg.

It's not the most rural it could be, but it's pretty rural. There are a lot of one-horse towns here. The town of Prospect does not even have one stoplight. There's probably fifteen churches, but no stoplights. There's a post office and two stores here. That's it. Farming is not as big as it was once, but there's a lot of farmland here, and there are a lot of people that still farm here for their livelihood.

I was born in the United Kingdom because my dad was in the military, and he was stationed in London. I came here when I was two, so I don't really remember it. I grew up in northern Virginia in Dale City, about thirty miles south of Washington, DC. It's very suburban. I never liked it since I was old enough to have an opinion about it. It's just very busy, a strip mall, commuters. When I left high school, I came to Richmond and lived there for about ten years, and then I spent some time on the West Coast. But—I think my whole journey was leading me here. This is my grandmother's property. When my mom retired, we came here together.

RAE: So you lived in Richmond, DC suburbs, and then on the West Coast.

ROBYN: Yeah, I lived in Tucson, Arizona, for a couple years, and I lived in San Diego, California, for a couple years.

RAE: So pretty much all cities before you moved here?

ROBYN: Correct.

RAE: That's interesting. I'm curious: If you'd spent that many years in cities, what made you want to move here? Did you have experiences in the country growing up, coming down here?

ROBYN: We used to come down to visit my grandmother when I was little. My sister and I used to spend the summers down here. Once, when I was living in Richmond, I decided I was going to move down here and raise ostriches. I had no money. I had no knowledge of ostriches. I just decided I was going to do it. Everybody remembers it, too. I'm like, "Do we really have to keep talking about the ostriches?"

RAE: Did you ever get ostriches?

ROBYN: No. I did not. I did not raise ostriches. I toured an ostrich farm. I know everything there is to know about ostriches, but I never raised any ostriches. It was just a dream.

RAE: Has it died? Are you over that dream?

ROBYN: No, I'm not really over it. I could have an ostrich. There are more practical things right now. My next thing that I'm going to get is probably pigs. But I should probably get an ostrich one day, just so I can be like, "I got an ostrich."

RAE: And so you can have an egg that big in your life.

ROBYN: Mm-hmm. Exactly, yeah.

RAE: I'm curious: When you were living in cities, were you always wishing you were in the country, or were you pretty content?

ROBYN: When I lived in cities, I thought I'd never not want to live there. I thought I'd live in a city forever unless I was independently wealthy, in which case I'd have a city home and a country home. I don't know if I matured or what happened, but I was living in San Diego and suddenly, after fourteen years of being away from my family, I was like, *I really want to be with my family*. I really hadn't been home, except for Thanksgiving and Christmas, for twelve years. I came home for Christmas that year, and I just decided. I said, "Mom, I'm coming home. I'm bringing the dog. We're moving in." I ended up living with my sister, her partner, her daughter, and my mom. We were all living in a townhouse, and I was like, *This is really overwhelming.* But then my mom retired, and we decided, this is her home place, so we moved down.

Like I said, I think my whole journey led me here. I wanted to be down here as a kid because I wanted to raise animals. That's how little kids think. I enjoyed all my other experiences, but now that I'm here I feel like I live in paradise. I hardly even leave to go on vacation. It's perfect. This is where I belong. I want to respect my family history, and I want to preserve this land. That became more important to me than living in a city. Don't get me wrong, it was a *huge* adjustment, and a huge culture shock. Pay is different. Things are very different here. Now I like to visit the city, but I don't want to stay there. I want to be here.

I feel a very strong commitment to this property that's been in my family for over a hundred years. My great-grandparents moved here from West Virginia and bought forty acres of land at the turn of the century. So, if you think about it, my great-grandfather would have been a Black man traveling from West Virginia at that time. Just wrap your head around that. He and my great-grandmother bought the land on credit. Out of the original forty acres, thirty-five are still here. My grandmother and her, I don't know, fourteen brothers and sisters were born here. My mom and her five brothers and sisters were born here. That wooden structure up there is the porch to the original farmhouse. It's important to me. There's a lot of history here.

This is Prince Edward County, Virginia. When they passed *Brown v. Board of Education* to integrate the school systems, Prince Edward County closed all the public schools because they didn't want to integrate. They opened some private schools for white students, and some churches got together to make scholarships for white students that couldn't afford to go to private schools, but the public schools were closed for five years. At the time, my mom was in grade school.

She and her brothers had to go stay with family elsewhere to go to school, if you can imagine that, as an elementary schooler. Plus they farmed here—sending your children away is sending your laborers away, you know what I mean?

There was a philanthropist who created a *Brown v. Board of Education* scholarship for people that were affected by the school closings. So, after retiring from thirty-five years with the federal government, she went back to school, just because she had the opportunity. She got a bachelor's degree in business administration. She never worked after. She did it just to do it. I think the experience of leaving when she was so young was pretty traumatic for her, so she never really discussed it until she was about to retire. Now she talks about it all the time. She thinks people should know that this happened, that we have this history in our country. When they were sent away for school, she said that her mom and her aunts were taking in laundry and cleaning people's houses to try to send money to the people that were taking care of the kids. They really tried. My grandparents were not educated people, but they did the best they could.

If you stand up in the gazebo there—like I said, that was the porch to the original farmhouse—those two trees there . . . that's the same view that every person in my family that's lived here over the years has had. When we first moved here, it was raining, and I went up and sat in the gazebo, and I was like, *Yeah, this is it. This is the ticket here. I'm happiest just being right here.*

Robyn was another narrator who taught me to let go of some of my rigidity or sense that I needed to keep interviews standardized and consistent, and instead she taught me to follow the conversation where it needed to go. Again and again, she told me that she'd never really had a problem with her queerness in the place she lived. And she returned to the importance of celebrating and carrying on histories of Black farming and land stewardship, and of supporting her mother and family in maintaining this land that had been in her family for generations. A few years ago, Robyn shared on social media that her mom had written a book about her life. I ordered a copy and loved learning more about Robyn's family history through her mother's memoir. You can hear more of Robyn's interview in season 1 of the podcast.

Tessa Eskander at the Highlander Center, New Market, Tennessee, November 2017

TESSA ESKANDER she/her, 21 years old

Anitsalagi (Cherokee), S'atsoyaha (Yuchi), and Šaawanwaki (Shawnee) lands
Cookeville, Tennessee
November 11, 2017

I met Tessa in fall 2017 at an Out in the South gathering at the Highlander Center—part of a series of gatherings organized by the Appalachian Community Fund and facilitated by my friend Kendall Billbrey (who is also one of the first country queers I interviewed in the summer of 2013) The gathering brought together queer and trans people from across central Appalachia and Tennessee. During the afternoon break before dinner, Tessa and I sat down in one of the dorm rooms near the workshop center.

TESSA: I'm from Cookeville, Tennessee. Born and raised. I went to elementary school, middle school, and high school. I even went to college there. I was hoping to go to a different place, but out-of-state tuition is ridiculous. So that was the reason I decided to stay there.

I am a transgender woman. Wooooo! I'm a chemical engineering student. I'm an Eagle Scout. Black Belt. Just lots of different things. I have an awesome boyfriend. I didn't come out until after I graduated high school and I was in college, because there wasn't really that good of a GSA

[Gender-Sexuality Alliance] at the time. It supposedly existed, but I never knew about it. So I was always really afraid of being out at the time, and I didn't realize how depressed I was until after I transitioned. But things are so much better now.

Coming out to my parents was rough to begin with, but, after a lot of long conversations and convincing them that conversion therapy and all that stuff was bad—like, for my dad, I showed him medical articles proving why that is wrong, and he was just like, "Oh, okay." And then, with my mom, she was trying to read Bible verses to me the second conversation we had, and I'm like, "You're not even Christian!"

They came around probably about six months later. They finally started to be like, "Okay, this is a thing," because I was already on hormones at that point and they were like, "It will be easier if we just accept it." They were not wanting to say my pronouns, and I was being obnoxious, like, "No, it's actually this." Every time they would mess it up, I would correct them, and they just got tired of hearing me correct them.

My mom initially said she never wanted to see me in a dress. Probably about eight months ago? She actually bought me a dress. We went to the store and she bought me a dress, and it was *such* a big deal. It's this white dress with blue stripes, and it's very floral. It's one of the nicest dresses I have, and it fits really well. I love it. So it is possible for your family to turn around; it just takes—it can take a while.

Currently I have blending privilege, so most people don't know I'm trans, which is part of the reason why I have my bumper sticker. It has the trans flag, and then in black lettering it says, "Transgender Woman" and "Eagle Scout" below it, and I get a bunch of weird looks. Most of them are just people giving me, like, head-twisted, really confused looks, 'cause they can't picture in their universe. So I think it's kind of fun.

This short excerpt captures a moment from Tessa's story that I just love. There was something so sweet in the way she recounted it. I remember the fluctuations in the tone of her voice and her laugh at the end. There are, of course, many queer and trans people whose relationships with their parents are changed forever, and sometimes completely broken, through the process of claiming their full and true selves. But I love the hopefulness in this story about Tessa's parents' evolution. You can hear more of Tessa's interview in season 1 of the podcast.

Silas House at the Hindman Settlement School, Hindman, Kentucky, July 2018

SILAS HOUSE he/him, 46 years old

S'atsoyaha (Yuchi), Šaawanwaki (Shawnee), and Adena lands
Berea, Kentucky
July 24, 2018

*I first met Silas at the Appalachian Writers'
Workshop in Hindman, Kentucky, in the
summer of 2013. I'm a huge fan of his novels
and other writing, and specifically his stories
depicting queer Appalachian lives, which
helped change the landscape of Appalachian
literature. In 2018, I was living just down the
road from Hindman in rural Knott County,
Kentucky, and though I wasn't attending
the workshop that summer, I asked Silas if I
could drive over and interview him. We pulled
two chairs together at the foot of the bed in
the room where he and his husband, Jason
Kyle Howard, were staying on the Hindman
Settlement School campus. I set the recorder
down on the bed and we got lost in talking and
almost missed dinner. After eating, we picked
up again right where we left off. Eastern
Kentucky lives beautifully in his words and
way of talking. Silas became Kentucky's first
openly gay poet laureate in 2023.*

SILAS: I was born in Whitley County,
Kentucky, which is right on the Tennessee–
Kentucky border, about an hour straight
north of Knoxville. I was raised in the
Holiness Church. My mother was, and still is,

a really beloved gospel singer. Even when we
weren't at our church for the three- or four-
hour services three or four nights a week, she
would sing at nursing homes or tent revivals,
camp meetings, or brush arbors. It's like our
whole lives revolved around church. From
the time I was eleven or twelve years old,
I started really questioning all that, which
was around the same time that I knew I was
gay. As I think back, that was really the only
bad part of my childhood, was knowing
that people in my family were incredibly
homophobic and that it was backed up by the
church, which was all-powerful. Other than
that, I had a wonderful childhood. I always
thought that everything was done in a big
way there. You didn't do anything halfway.
You loved really big and loud, and you
fought really big and loud, and everything in
between. I'm really thankful for all of that,
the good and the bad. It was an interesting,
complex place to grow up.

I don't hear people talk enough
about the way that the AIDS epidemic
held a whole generation of people from
coming out. Besides the religion, also that
consciousness and awareness of AIDS really
held me back from thinking that there
might be a possibility of me living a gay
life—mostly because I knew the way my
parents would react to it. I thought I would

be dead to them. I thought I would lose my whole family, and I couldn't fathom that. I had grown up in such a tight family. It was just drilled into us that family, blood, was the only thing that mattered. I had friends in high school growing up, but the main core was your cousins. You were to be at family gatherings no matter what. It was just that Scots-Irish clannishness. It was in our DNA. I would often think, *Would I rather be happy in* this *way, or happy in* this *way? Or, stay in the closet and be sad because I can't be with somebody I really want to be with, or be out and be sad because I can't be with my family?* The way I often thought of it was coming out would have been putting myself before other people, which was the number one thing I had been taught to never do, to always be selfless.

I had a relationship with a male boss who was twelve years older than me. That went on for maybe four years or so, from the time I was seventeen until about the end of college, and it was very sporadic. That was the only person I'd ever had any kind of gay relationship with at all. Then, after I got to college—this sounds so stupid, but it was the way I thought at the time—I thought, *I really want the American dream. I want the picket fence, and I want kids, and I want all of that.* I couldn't have fathomed a gay family

at that time; that would've never seemed possible to me. Again, I think a lot of that is representation. I just never saw anything like that. At that point, every gay character that you saw was suffering. They were miserable. If there was a gay character in a movie, he was bound to die of AIDS or suicide. I really wanted a family. I was dating this woman who was really beautiful and smart. We had a good relationship. I thought that would work. Just to make a long story short, we had two children, we were married thirteen years, but it just didn't work out.

During that time, I put so much of myself into writing. All of the suffering I had about being gay, all the confusion I had, and the guilt. I had guilt about everything. I was raised Holiness. It's like being raised Catholic; you feel guilty about everything. I put that all into writing. My first three books, they're all about guilt. And I put everything into my kids. I was over-the-top involved as a father. I always had one with me. People would say to me, "You're more like a mother than a father," because of those gender norms about mothers and fathers. I just always had them with me, and most men didn't do that in our culture. I took them to work, I took them on the road.

I just resigned myself. I remember one day thinking, *I'll never really have a true*

great love of my life, but my kids are the loves of my life. Then, at a certain point, I realized that's really not fair to put that on them. I thought about that for a long time. I went through a long process. Then I met Jason, who was just such an incredible love. I knew immediately that he was everything that I'd always wanted. That's when I really started to examine myself and think, *What is the best thing for my children?* It was also almost to the point where if I didn't become who I really was, I was afraid I wasn't going to survive it.

Eventually I just thought, *This love is too huge to let go. I just can't do it.* I came out to everybody when I was thirty-four. It didn't go well at all with my parents. It took them about ten years. Now they're great. They're really accepting of Jason. They love him. They come to our house, eat supper, and sit around on the porch. Jason and my father work on projects together. They repaired

the roof the other day together. Every time I see something like that, I'm like, *God, am I really able to have both things?* I keep waiting for the bottom to drop out. I think there's something in the way that I was raised that things can't be that good. Not that we have perfect lives or anything. Of course, bad things happen, and trouble, but the things I always wanted were to have somebody that I was really able to love completely, in every way, and also to have my family. I've been able to have that over the last two or three years. It's just the most amazing peace to have that, and for my children to love Jason. We now have that family that I never thought could exist. It still is mind-boggling to me.

Silas's writing and teaching have been a gift to so many Appalachian and southern readers and writers. He helped carve a doorway for more queer mountain writers to step through after him. He's truly a legend, a sweet and thoughtful Leo (with excellent hair) and someone I admire greatly. You can hear more of our interview in season 1 of the podcast, and you can find interviews, articles, and more featuring Silas's work online.

Dorothy Allison at home in Guerneville, California, August 2018

DOROTHY ALLISON she/her, 69 years old

Kashia, Coast Miwok, Southern Pomo, and Graton Rancheria lands
Guerneville, California
August 2, 2018

For many, Dorothy Allison needs no introduction. She is the working-class, lesbian, southern writer who cleared a path for those coming up behind her. I don't have room here to describe how important her writing has been, and continues to be, in my life.

In 2018, I was awarded a scholarship to a writing workshop in Washington State, where I was signed up to be in her novel class, but due to health issues, she couldn't make it. I got a wild hair and wrote her a gushing fan letter on Instagram, of all places. I told her I was going to be in California for a community radio conference later that year, and asked if she'd be up for an interview. She gave me the landline number for her house, and I still remember her partner, Alix, answering the phone, the pause while she went to get Dorothy, and then there was Dorothy on the other end of the line.

I rented a car and drove all the way across California, west to east, and showed up on her doorstep. She gave me a tour of her yard—wearing a sunflower visor and walking with a cane. She fed me a plum from the tree in her backyard and talked about the redwoods looming overhead, and then we sat down at the patio table under thick shade. I was so nervous and starstruck I could barely talk, and at the same time she felt so familiar to me. I have joked to friends since that she topped

the hell out of that interview. After I fumbled my way through the first couple questions, she took charge and guided our conversation.

DOROTHY: We moved up here because I had to get the fuck out of San Francisco or I was going to die. I have a tendency to push myself to collapse anyway, and I was doing it with such profound intensity that I would probably have managed to do myself more damage than I did. And I wasn't that good at urban life, because I'm largely a hermit. I don't like the noise, and I don't like the density in city life.

So we moved up here; one, to raise our son. I don't know how the fuck that happened. I married a woman who wanted a baby, and I thought, *I can always leave.* I didn't realize that I would fall in love with the baby. I knew I was in love with her. When you find a dangerous-looking/acting but intensely loving butch, it's kind of amazing. It's like, *Hold me down, honey, but not too hard.* I had never known that you could say "not too hard"! Alix was . . . extraordinary. It's been a good, solid, long-term relationship. I find it really awkward to realize we've been together for thirty-one years. We used to date girls together . . . kinky! But that got to be too exhausting, and they would fall in love with one or the other of us. It was just too complicated, so we don't do that anymore. We flirt, but don't follow through.

Then life takes you up, and there is always something that needs doing. I mean, I know [Donald] Trump is worse than almost anything we've had to deal with in the last sixty years of my life, but there is always some crazy fucker. Before Trump, there was Jerry Falwell. It's the same old, same old. Even now, we're still not acceptable. They still want to get rid of us and/or force us to assume a pretense of not being who we are. I think that's the issue, of course. They don't care if we fuck each other; we're just supposed to be ashamed of ourselves and do it in private. And I'm not ashamed of myself.

RAE: Do you ever miss the South?

DOROTHY: I do.

RAE: What are things you miss about the South?

DOROTHY: Biscuits. People who know how to make a decent biscuit. People who know how to season a pan of beans. You go to all these

"southern" restaurants in New York City and San Francisco, or in fucking Sonoma County, and they are just *pathetic*. Pathetic! They're uncomfortable with pork. Well, let me just say you can't make beans without pork that taste worth a damn! All these vegetarians make my teeth hurt!

I do miss the South. I miss the smell. I've gone and done residencies at various colleges in Georgia, North Carolina, and Mississippi. It's a little tricky because you are their token queer and you're acceptable because you're mildly famous, and they're not sure how dangerous you are until you show them. But I'm very, very clear that, to a large extent, it's about tokenization. I might be acceptable, but if I shaved my head, I wouldn't be. I know these things. And I keep track of the disdain that people express for other queer writers, and I don't work with them.

Also the thing I should say is, you run yourself into the ground as steadily as I have for most of my life, and you will pay for it. I had a complete metabolic collapse a few years ago, and I couldn't digest food. Christ, I lost fifty pounds in five months and couldn't walk and had to redesign my life. I had to learn to sleep. Writing requires so much focus and intensity. I'd be working, and I would have to get up and walk back and forth and swing my arms in the air just to burn off some of the emotional energy that gets triggered with writing. That will, long term, have some impact.

But writing is magic. It works sometimes, and other times it doesn't, and you're fucked. You just got to somehow survive the process and try to enjoy it if you can. I like writing. I don't like publishing. I don't like becoming an icon. It's uncomfortable. But the system that we have in place, of lauding some people and disdaining others, assumes that some people know more. I'm not convinced that's the case. Some of us just got more endurance.

I don't know that writing is healing . . . but I do think that the work of being able to write—and that means being able to think about your life and the lives of people you love—that work is a great curative for self-hatred. I was raised to hate myself. Most women in the South are. And I had to figure out that was not necessary, that I could live a different kind of life.

You think that because you're lesbian that you are short-circuiting that whole system. But no, it's still there. Jesus Christ, I was raised in the Baptist church! There is no worse environment for a sane female human being, because you are raised to sacrifice yourself completely. You are raised to be in service to other people. To believe yourself valid, to believe yourself worthy of being loved, to believe yourself sufficient in and of yourself doesn't go along with being raised in the Baptist church. Of course, I was a damn fool and fell in love with a Mormon. They're even worse. God *save* me!

But I don't believe in this California self-love nonsense either. I believe in Ursula Le Guin. I want to be a grown-up. I want to be a responsible citizen. I want to be an up-front and matter-of-fact member of my community, and I want to make it clear what I have survived and what it has cost to survive it. I've got a fuck lot of cousins who died, mostly killed themselves in stupid, stupid ways. Not just liquor and drugs, but fast cars and violent lovers and despair. Poverty is the inculcator of despair. No. I don't intend to ever participate or support a system that makes that the norm. I've got two sisters I've watched barely survive, and neither of them graduated from high school. Out of my thousands of cousins, there are six of us who graduated from high school and went to college. Five graduated from college. We are the grease that makes the engines of America run. We're the working class.

And me, I'm just a runaway. But we do interesting work, us queer runaways.

At the time of this interview, I was experiencing an active flare-up of ulcerative colitis, traveling while also deeply anemic and fatigued. Dorothy's warnings about the long-term health implications of running yourself into the ground year after year landed hard. I felt like she was speaking directly to my experience, though I hadn't told her anything about my chronic illness or increasing inability to juggle as many projects as I had been over the preceding few years. I return to this interview often, for writing advice, for inspiration, and because I adore that line about the wonders of "a dangerous-looking/acting but intensely loving butch." You can hear more of Dorothy's interview in season 2 of the podcast.

THE PANDEMIC ERA

2020-2023

In January 2020—burnt out on my community radio job and desperate to find a way to spend a few months working full time on Country Queers for the first time ever—I launched another Kickstarter campaign to raise money to produce season 1 of the *Country Queers* podcast. We had an in-person Extravagaynza at Appalshop in eastern Kentucky, where I worked at the time, which included the second gallery opening of the exhibit, along with live music and drag performances. The Kickstarter campaign was not just fully funded; we exceeded our goal, and I gave notice at my job that I'd leave in April of that year.

In March 2020, with the entire country and much of the world suddenly locked down due to COVID-19, I thought, *I must be absolutely nuts to quit a full-time job with only $6,000 in the bank in such uncertain times.* That $6,000, raised via Kickstarter, was needed to pay myself and my friend Tommy Anderson (who was living in a camper with their dog Goo in the yard of the house I rented at the time) to work on producing an eight-episode podcast season, which we'd promised to start releasing in June. But after seven years of inching the project along during free time outside full-time work or school, fretting about how we'd ever get these stories out in a way that was accessible to other isolated rural queer people, and deep exhaustion from trying to move this project forward while navigating ever-worsening chronic illness, fatigue, and nonprofit burnout, I took the jump. I had no job lined up after August, when all the Kickstarter funds were slated to run out. But I also felt that if I didn't take the risk, these interviews might sit in my hard drive forever.

I knew I needed a team of folks to help me think through the decisions I was making: which narrators to include in our first season, which sections of their interviews to feature, and how to situate individual personal narratives in the context of the time each was recorded as well as the realities of the summer of 2020: a time of mass unemployment and housing crises, a raging global pandemic, uprisings in response to the police murders of George Floyd and Breonna Taylor, and intense uncertainty about the future.

I reached out to three friends whose work and brains I greatly admire: hermelinda cortés, who was Southerners on New Ground (SONG)'s communications director for many years; Sharon P. Holland, professor of critical race, queer, and feminist theory at UNC Chapel Hill; and Lewis Raven Wallace, a journalist I worked with at *Scalawag* magazine—and the only person I knew who had produced a narrative podcast. I asked each of them if they'd be willing to serve on a volunteer editorial advisory team, assuming they'd say no because they're extremely busy. They all replied with enthusiastic yesses.

Season 1, which rolled out in the summer of 2020, features edited interviews I had recorded up until that point. The editorial team worked with me to craft host narration that introduced listeners to the project and to the context of the interview, but that also positioned the interviews in a larger political and historical context. We decided to include a call to action in the middle of each episode, asking our white listeners with access to wealth to commit to a process of reparations by donating to land and wellness projects led by queer and trans people who are Black, Indigenous, and People of Color. With our mostly volunteer team scattered across three states, and a terrible internet connection on my end, we produced nine full episodes in three months—no small feat. But it was incredible to get to see other rural queer people interacting with these oral histories. In retrospect, I think the podcast was born at exactly the right time. In the middle of a global pandemic defined by collective isolation, we began releasing stories and interviews full of wisdom from rural and small-town LGBTQIA2S+ narrators—

many of whom had already been navigating isolation for decades.

For the first time, it felt like people were really listening and starting to realize that rural queer people and this little DIY central Appalachian–based oral history project had some important things to say. To me, the success of this effort is measured by the fact that that summer, messages poured in via email and social media from rural and small-town LGBTQIA2S+ people all over who shared that they found comfort and connection in those episodes. At the same time, during this chapter of the project's story (and the previous two as well), I was navigating an ongoing cyberstalking experience that lasted an incredibly stressful seven years. At times frightening, and largely unfolding behind the scenes, the experience made my personal relationship to visibility through the Country Queers project quite fraught.

As the pandemic continued into winter, I had lost three friends in three months, and I found myself extremely isolated and depressed. I lived alone in a dark house at the head of a holler with an increasing mold and rat problem, while on immunosuppressants for an autoimmune disease. Out of pure desperation to find some joy in those gray cold days, I started recording virtual phone and video interviews with other country queers who love sheep. I ended up producing a fun three-part series called *Ode to Sheep*. In late 2020, thanks to a contract radio-production gig I picked up immediately after season 1 ended, I bought a thirty-by-eight-foot vintage Spartan camper, arranged to rent land from childhood friends in West Virginia, and asked another family friend to haul the camper up a steep, narrow mountain road into a high hay field. I moved back to West Virginia from Kentucky in early February 2021 with two pregnant goats, two dogs, twelve ducks, an elderly, blind, one-eyed cat, and all my plants, books, and belongings. My friends Ada Smith and Jacob Mack-Boll helped me move, forming a three-vehicle caravan, with the animals divided between my truck and Ada's car. There was no gravel on the driveway up the hill to the camper, so, on a cold winter evening just before dark, we used a wheelbarrow to move the basics we needed out of the U-Haul and up the steep driveway. The ducks disappeared into the briars at dusk, but somehow, we got all but one back into their makeshift house I'd built out of scrap tin and wood before it was too dark to see. We all slept in the camper and awoke the next morning to a stunning and heavy wet snow—and also no electricity. I spent my first week in the camper with no

power or heat, continuing to move in by pushing wheelbarrow load after wheelbarrow load up a steep hill, with an ulcerative colitis flare raging and only an outhouse. The power came back in a few days, but I had no water for the first five weeks I lived here. Even still, I woke up every morning excited to look out the window at these mountains, giddy to finally be starting a life I'd dreamed of for at least fifteen years: a little home of my own in the West Virginia mountains, with dairy goats and some time to write.

Since then, I've managed to mostly make ends meet without going back to full-time nonprofit work. I've juggled freelance writing, audio production, and copywriting jobs that ebb and flow. I've worked at the gift shop for the national park nearby selling postcards and magnets to tourists. I've spoken on virtual panels at colleges and online movement spaces. Country Queers received a Southern Power Fund award in late 2020 and a Queer Mobilization Fund grant in early 2021, which made it possible to pay myself to work on the project full time for nine months and allowed us to produce an experimental, collaborative second season over the course of that year. We teamed up with Out in the Open—a Vermont-based organization working to build rural LGBTQ power in the Northeast—and invited six community participants from our networks to join us in some virtual skill shares around oral history interviewing and audio recording. Those community participants then recorded interviews and worked with the *Country Queers* podcast team and Out in the Open staff to produce episodes. Season 2 includes stunning phone and video interviews, audio diaries, and conversations between rural and small-town queer and trans folks in Vermont, Kentucky, Georgia, Mississippi, Texas, and Hawai'i. It features gorgeous sound design by Ren Tokui and music by queer and trans musicians across the South. That season, I hired Vick Quezada as Country Queers' social media artist and manager and paid them from our small but steady monthly income from memberships on Patreon.

Some people think that making a podcast is quick and easy work, and that is true for some shows. But, in the case of *this* podcast— from relationship building, conducting interviews, transcription, editing first and second cuts, multiple check-ins for consent from narrators to back-and-forth edits with editorial advisors, sound design and mixing, scheduling, release, and promotion—we have easily poured hundreds of hours into each episode. Despite the financial support that came through for season 2, it's still a bit of a miracle we pulled off an eight-part collaborative, multi-time-zone podcast of this scale, while paying stipends to community participants, wages to our sound designer,

Queens of Queen City, Cumberland, Maryland, June 2022

musicians, and myself as producer and showrunner, and (very small) honorariums to the editorial team.

During this time, my chronic illness also flared up badly. I couldn't get broadband internet at home, so I was doing extensive media uploading and Zoom videoconferences from the hotspot on my phone. And once again, in the middle of this complicated cross-country experiment to collaboratively produce a podcast season by and for rural and small-town LGBTQIA2S+ people, all of whom had challenges with cell service and internet, I was without water for another month and a half due to a dried-up spring in late summer. Plus, I was continuing to try to build out and maintain the infrastructure on the hillside where I live: constructing a porch with my dad and brother, which doubled my covered living space; constantly fighting my solar electric fence in an attempt to contain the goats; milking the goats, making cheese, washing duck eggs, and trying to keep up with mowing without being able to afford a mower of my own. It was *a lot*. It still is, honestly. But season 2 turned out beautifully.

During these past several years of societal reflection and reckoning around racism and colonization in the United States, long-standing questions around my role leading this project came front and center for me.

In season 1, in the context of a project that deals so deeply with stories about place, agriculture, and land, questions loomed around how to think and talk about Black and Indigenous histories and presents without editorializing or adding my own thoughts and politics into narrators' accounts of their deeply personal experiences. In season 2, many of those questions continued during our collaborative experiment. The volume was turned up on major questions about the project's financial and energetic sustainability as well. While the project received an infusion of much-needed financial support during the pandemic, it has not guaranteed its (or my own) ongoing financial stability. Burning questions remain about the long-term sustainability of this project, and yet, a deep commitment to and love for documenting our long-silenced histories remains.

Also, chronic illness is a bitch.

In the section ahead, you might notice that the interviews take a bit of a turn away from the format and focus of previous sections. Something about that pandemic portal unlocked greater flexibility, curiosity, and lack of worry about consistency in my interviewing approach. You'll meet five narrators who take us into the worlds of raising alpaca, drag performance, and more.

Penelope Logue and some of the herd. Photo courtesy of Penelope Logue

PENELOPE LOGUE she/her, 40 years old

Tsitsistas (Cheyenne), and Núuchi-u (Ute) lands
Westcliffe, Colorado
January 5, 2021

In the midst of the first full winter of the COVID-19 pandemic, I was, like many of us, in desperate need of some joy. On Twitter, I saw a video of a cute kid in England showing a sheep via video, since in-person sheep shows were canceled, and I got to thinking about how I'd never heard a radio story featuring sheep, despite the fact that they're very auditorily engaging. I made a post on Country Queers socials to see if any other queer and trans people who love sheep wanted to talk to me on the phone for a spontaneous bonus episode. I heard back from almost two dozen folks, and through terrible cell service and internet quality on both ends, I recorded a dozen phone and video calls about gender, sexuality, land, farming, and . . . sheep! One of the folks I met was Penelope Logue, cofounder of the Tenacious Unicorn Ranch. You can hear more of this conversation in "Ode to Sheep: Part Two."

PENELOPE: My name is Penelope Logue, I'm in Westcliffe, Colorado, and I am an alpaca rancher. I run the Tenacious Unicorn Ranch. We're a queer haven and an active ranch that started about two and a half years ago.

I grew up on a farm in Longmont, Colorado. I was adopted by my maternal grandparents, and my adoptive mom and dad were computer programmers. But my dad grew up in the Depression era, where you didn't do just one thing. So we had a fully active farm on top of his programming. We didn't keep animals, but I wanted to, desperately. I was in 4-H, and our neighbors had animals, and I would go take care of them. So I learned all of my animal husbandry from that era of my life.

I grew up in a Christian home, which didn't make being queer publicly possible. Oh, by the way, I identify as queer. I'm a trans woman; my pronouns are she/her. I was born in 1980, and there wasn't language—or at least language that would have filtered down to me in podunk Longmont, Colorado—that would have given me the ability to come out. And I grew up in a Southern Baptist and Greek Orthodox home. So I was in church three days a week, minimum. As soon as I started hitting puberty and making sexual decisions, or, like, leaning one way or the other, I was sent to camp to get that out of me. Because I was presenting male then, of course, and I was very attracted to men, and that was disallowed heavily—although my parents were on the more liberal end of conservatism, if that makes sense. They loved me to death and wanted what was best for me, and they were trying to do that in their pursuit of me being at least not stand-out gay. There was no word to describe being transgender back then. There was no way I could have communicated that to them, although I tried. I think that a lot of people my age tried desperately in their teenage years to convey what was going on, and it just wasn't received.

I got married and had a kid at eighteen, and then I joined the military because making ends meet was very difficult. That was during Don't Ask, Don't Tell,* and I was a combat arms during the onset of the Iraq War. I don't talk about my military career, so we can just skip over that period of my life. I got out of the military, and I was—in a lot of ways—lost for a long time. I tried various things. I was a help desk manager for IBM for a while. I was a barista for a while, which I thoroughly enjoyed. Then I got my broker's license, and I was a broker for a long time.

I should say: right after I got out of the military, I had another child with a girl that lives in Oregon. And my child came out as trans. They're nonbinary. So that started

me down the path of realizing that I had issues that I needed to cope with. In trying to create a safe environment for a trans child to just go to school, I learned a lot about the inequalities that affect queer people. Because I'm white. I have blonde hair and blue eyes, and up until that point I had not faced a lot of adversity in my life. But trying to just get my child educated without it being a risk to their life was kind of an awakening for me.

I sought counseling for my PTSD [posttraumatic stress disorder], and through that counseling I was able to open all of those doors that I had shut in my teenage years. So then I came out fully as transgender, and that's where I mark my life beginning. I kind of hit the ground running. I've always been a little bit of an activist, but I really stepped up my activism for basic equality for trans people, and ecologically speaking, we're tilting over an edge that matters so, so fucking much.

Then, I had to move out of my house, because I was living in Commerce City in Denver and the threats became routine. I was in fear of my life, like, *really.* So I moved back to Longmont, and I got a job

* For more on the Clinton-era "Don't Ask, Don't Tell" legislation, see Ali Rogan, "How Don't Ask, Don't Tell Has Affected LGBTQ Service Members, 10 Years after Repeal," PBS, December 22, 2020, https://www.pbs.org/newshour/nation/how-dont-ask-dont-tell-has-affected-lgbtq-service-members-10-years-after-repeal.

at Target. I just wanted to heal a little bit and have no pressure. Being a broker comes with an extreme amount of pressure, and I was waiting to get surgeries and stuff. I was a line manager at Target and really kind of experimenting with dating for the first time and all these other things—like going through my second teenage years, as it were.

Then Trump got elected. And, I mean, having watched societies collapse firsthand, I saw all of the warning signs that was Trumpism. So I started gathering good people around me, and I started the process of selling my house in Denver in order to make a haven, a safe place for queer people. It was kind of reactionary. "We've got to do something!" Then, an opportunity to rent a ranch in Livermore, Colorado, came up. So we rented forty acres there. I had wanted alpaca for a minute but never could justify getting alpaca. I had been talking to a couple that was retiring, and their herd was becoming a little bit too much for them, but they wanted it to stay together. So I inherited seventy-two alpacas from this couple. Then, from there, the Tenacious Unicorn Ranch was born in October 2018. We've just been running forward ever since, trying to make it work. We have 186 head of alpaca right now.

RAE: How did you get interested in alpaca?

Had you ever been around them before?

PENELOPE: It's this weird thing, right? I had never been introduced to alpaca, but at my church, when I was about seven or eight, there was a family that was doing missionary work in Peru, and they brought back photos of these fucking mythical creatures called alpaca. I had never seen anything like that in my life. My mom is Armenian and so camels, sure! I understand a camel. But an alpaca is like an *adorable* camel! It's everything you want a camel to be! It's furrier, and shorter, and not as threatening, and adorable! In Peru at the festivals, they dress them up, and I had never met one, but they were just fascinating to me. It was kind of always in the back of my mind, like, *Alpaca! If I could ever make that work . . .* And now I have two hundred of them!

RAE: We had llamas when I was growing up, and I never got spit on, but there was one that spit on my mom a couple times. Do the alpaca spit?

PENELOPE: Oh yeah. People get weird around animals spitting on them. You learn right away when you start with alpaca that it's not saliva that they're spitting at you. It's actually regurgitation. It is essentially bile, and it smells thusly. I have been coated in it many times. It's their way of being like, "Fuck off," you know? They just start spitting. It's a very clear message, the most direct you can get. And yeah, it's gross, but also, it's just part of who they are and how they communicate. It's a way for them to let you know that they're uncomfortable or scared with what you're doing or what's going on.

Some of them never spit at all, like, ever. And then I have alpaca where spitting is their *go-to* move. It's how they say hi. When they're happy, they spit. When they're mad, they spit. And, you know, you love them all the same! But yeah, it's pretty vile. It has a smell that doesn't ever truly wash out of your clothes, and you just kind of deal with it. An alpaca does not care. Like, they will look you in the eye and spit directly in your mouth. And it is ten levels of gross, but it's just grass, at the end of the day. It's well-fermented grass. You paid for it! You might as well enjoy it! [*Laughs*]

There are many moments from this conversation with Penelope that I'm grateful for, and the deep dive into the details of raising alpaca was both fascinating and hilarious. There was a moment where Penelope imitated the various vocal sounds alpaca make that had me crying tears of laughter.

Since our interview in early 2021, the Tenacious Unicorn Ranch has relocated. I don't know the details, but I know that they had been posting about increased harassment and pressure from armed local folks prior to the move.

Suzanne Pharr at home in her garden, Little Rock, Arkansas. Photo courtesy of Renée DeLapp

SUZANNE PHARR she/her, 82 years old

Wahzhazhe (Osage), O-gah-pah (Quapaw), and Očhéthi Šakówiŋ (Oglala Sioux) lands
Little Rock, Arkansas
July 10, 2021

Suzanne Pharr is a badass southern, queer feminist and antiracist organizer and writer. I first shared space with Suzanne at the SONG Gaycation in East Tennessee in the summer of 2013. I would cross paths with her a handful of times over the next several years and was always intimidated by her quiet fierceness and political sharpness. I had dreamed of interviewing her for a long time but had been too shy to ask. So when the opportunity arose to interview her for an oral history project organized by the National Council of Elders (NCOE), I jumped at it. We were scheduled to talk via videoconference for two hours, but that stretched into four.

SUZANNE: Little Rock, Arkansas, is where I have spent a large portion of my life, coming here in 1973, and then being away for about ten years, and then coming back now to live. The community I live in feels like a small town, even though I can look at the state capitol from my back porch. It's a quadrant of about eight blocks in two directions. And it's quiet. It's slow. People talk to each other. We have trees. We try to keep our yards nice. But it feels like the country in terms of the social environment.

But where I call home is . . . probably so many places, but it's always out in the natural world, and I think that's because the deep center of home for me was a farm. I grew up in rural Georgia, which is now urban Georgia. It was only this year that our family farm was sold and will be turned into a housing development. So it's been a tremendous sense of loss and tragedy. When I grew up, it was six miles to the closest town, and then another forty-five minutes or so into Atlanta. It was out in the farmland of North Georgia, in a place called Hog Mountain.

That was a place where I had tremendous freedom. I think partly because we had such a big family, we had so many things that we were each responsible for, and we had some acreage that we could run on. It was about eighty acres; maybe fifty of that was in farmland. So from the time I was very, very little, every moment I could, I was either in the woods playing or in the barn playing. These were the great loves for me. My older three siblings were girls, and then the next four were boys. The common joke in our family is "We have three girls, four boys, and Suzanne." It took me a long time to understand what that meant in terms of gender.

I played with animals all the time. I was a solitary kind of kid within a big family. Not a lonely kid. I had plenty of attention. But I just loved, *loved* animals, and I loved that outside world. I think a good example of it is—you know how moss grows on the north side of trees? Well, in Georgia, at that time, it was a very beautiful, soft moss, and you would get patches of moss that were maybe a foot in breadth and a foot in depth. And I would create worlds in that, using acorns, using all the little things that were around me. I'd create little towns, little places where my imaginary animals and real animals might live. So that's the kind of joy that it gave me to live on a farm. And I loved farming. I love what we did. I love the fields, I love seeing things grow, and bringing things in. I have no complaints whatsoever about growing up on a farm.

In terms of gender, I identify as queer. But I mostly define myself by my political work. Otherwise, I've defined myself as a reader, a person who clings pretty closely to books. I define myself as a social justice worker, a writer, and organizer. I'd put "organizer" before "writer" because I didn't write until I realized this was something I could do and that needed to be done to document and explain to myself and others what was happening as we roared through the seventies, and eighties and onward. I call myself a political handywoman, because I have just been in so many organizations and so many different kinds of work on different kinds of issues.

There's nothing like community. When I think of social units, I think whatever we choose to call family sits at the center of it. And I have, for a very long time, urged a redefinition of family. To move it absolutely out of the hierarchal and gendered form that it's in now. To spread it. Spread it just as wide as it can be and to nourish it. Nourish it from within and nourish it from without. I keep saying that queers are kind of experts on family because we've had to create our own, over and over. That may be breaking shape, changing a little bit now, with more conventional families accepting queers.

But we really need to break it open. To understand that it's not about *who* the people are; it's *what* we are to each other. Is it a configuration where people think that everyone is of equal worth, where we support one another, where we challenge one another, where we're bonded in it by a sense that we're in this together, and where we acknowledge each other? I think, particularly, feminist queers have done a really good job of shifting ideas around family. Just think of a zillion ways families are formed now, you know?

But . . . are they families when they don't speak? When they drop a child off to spend time with the other parent and don't even go to the door? You know, what's the family? Or is it a family where the woman is being abused every day? Or where the kid is being abused? Is that family?

So we need to come to a different way of talking about, thinking about, and acknowledging family. It is important. Because it is fractured, and for it to center around marriage is a loss. Instead of tightening the form, we should broaden the form of family. Benefits shouldn't be connected to whether you're married or not. We went to a domesticating victory with marriage equality, as opposed to one that radicalized and changed the whole idea of family. But it did bring a lot of recognition to people.

But anyway, it starts with family, and then the larger configuration is community, and then it goes out from there. So, back to what I would want to tell those younger organizers. The words I would want them to really hold tight to are "collectivity" and "cooperation." How do you build that? And it's not performative. And it's not just protest. Protest is a very powerful, powerful tool, but it is only a tool. It's not the hard work. It's the dangerous work. Getting five friends to go downtown and protest and put themselves in danger is an important thing. And it builds power, if you build on that. But it can't be just protest.

I'd say to other rural queers . . . go ahead and come out, if you possibly can, and just deal with that. I think one of the questions here was "Do you have any regrets?" I think that it would have been so much better for me if I had come out in college. Instead, it was a period of time when . . . I was not my whole self. I was fine. People thought I was a really good teacher. My family thought . . . I don't know what they thought, they thought I was odd. But I was in a battle over my sexuality or my politics. So it just meant that I always presented this person that wasn't fully me, and I think that's not good for you. I think that you only have *this much* life, you know? So I say no matter what you face, find your friends. Find . . . maybe that old man down the road who sits on the porch of the grocery store, you know? Find the people that you can talk to, and then gradually move out of secrecy. And I know, so many people leave, but I think that now there are more ways to have that conversation. I think when you feel like you're the only person in town, it's really, really hard. But you just have to find someone that you can hold a little bit safely to your heart and get involved in something that cherishes queerness and how fun our people can be.

Suzanne and I had a long list of questions to work from that had been developed by the NCOE oral history and podcast team (of which I am a proud member). We probably only made it through a handful of those, and I kept having to restrain myself from asking her all sorts of questions about her country queer life. After years of knowing who she was and a bit about her work, somehow that interview, virtual though it was, solidified a connection between us. I feel a kind of fierce kinship with her whose depth belies our brief in-person time together. In an email this summer, she called me her "heart-friend," and I think that's the best description. Her descriptions of growing up on a farm, spending most of her time outside with the animals, and building little homes out of logs and moss and sticks in the woods are exactly how I describe the best parts of my childhood. Also, I resonate intensely with her critique of heteronormativity and wishes for more expansive definitions and expressions of queer family.

A Polaroid photo of us, by alyzza may, at Haley Farm in Clinton, Tennessee, at a National Council of Elders gathering. When I showed it to Suzanne, she said, "Bug eyes and no eyes."

Kijana West on the porch of her apartment in Cumberland, Maryland, June 2022

KIJANA WEST she/her, 47 years old

Šaawanwaki (Shawnee) and Massawomeck lands
Cumberland, Maryland
June 7, 2022

In June 2022, I traveled north to the small city of Cumberland, Maryland, which sits in the mountains near the border with northern West Virginia. I was working on a story about a community of drag queens, fondly referred to as the Queens of Queen City for the Virginia Quarterly Review. *I spent eight days there, following the queens through their week of Pride festivities with photographer Mike Snyder. I recorded formal sit-down oral history interviews with many of the queens and also behind-the-scenes conversations in dressing rooms, parking lots, and alleyways. I was intrigued by Kijana's story. She was an active member of the Pride committee, and I was impressed by the range and scale of five days of events organized across Allegany County. I asked if I could interview her before I left town at the end of a long week of recording. We sat down on beach chairs on the porch of the apartment she rented at the time and talked for a couple hours as a light summer rain fell.*

KIJANA: I was born and raised in New York City. Born in Harlem, raised in Harlem and the Bronx. I went to private school pretty much all my life. I am a statistic. I was a teen mother. I got pregnant at fifteen, because of peer pressure. At that point, I already knew that I was gay, but I didn't have an outlet. Even though my mother was the head of the HIV department at Harlem Hospital, which was new back then. She was part of the fight against the AIDS epidemic. She was in the thick of it when it was really bad, and people didn't know what it was and they were calling it "the gay cancer." My mother was already out there. Working it, you know what I'm saying?

So I was kind of in the community because my mother was a social worker. However, I felt like I couldn't really get into that community because, one, I wasn't old enough. I knew that my mother had gay friends, queer friends, and I loved hanging out with them, but I didn't see anybody my age. And even though I went to school downtown in the Village, and I hung out on the pier, I always associated the pier, like—*Oh, man, I'm not homeless. My mother hasn't kicked me out yet, because she doesn't know. So I don't know if I fit in here.* Even though New York is a big city. . . I just didn't see anybody. I was still in a bubble. I went to school, and I came home. I didn't even hang out in my neighborhood because it wasn't safe. When I was growing up, I was watching prostitutes having sex in the back of their car outside of my bedroom window. I'm born in 1974, so this is New York in the eighties, okay? When crack was really crack. Like, it was a bad time. So I wasn't allowed to hang out in my neighborhood.

I had my daughter when I was sixteen. All of my friends were having sex with boys; I was the only one who wasn't, and I was afraid to come out to my friends. So the first time I had sex with a guy I got pregnant. So it was like, *That's it. I'm done. This is not for me.* I felt like my body had betrayed me.

My mother was really proactive at giving me the birds-and-the-bees talk. I knew at five that there's a vagina and a penis and there's sperm. But I just didn't feel comfortable. I didn't feel like I had an outlet. I got involved with an older woman, and my first sexual experience with a woman was at seventeen—this was after I had my daughter—and I think that person at the time was maybe ten years older than me. So my mother wasn't happy about that. I told my mother I was going to somebody's house for a slumber party. And I don't know how she even found the woman's number, but she called her. It was, like, six o'clock in the morning. And she was like, "I know you're at this person's house, and I know what you're doing. And I know you're sleeping with her. You need to come home now so we can talk about it." And

I was like, *Damn, my mother outed me!* You know what I mean? Then, when it came out that I was gay, the response from my family was wild, because most of them were not surprised. I felt like an idiot, because I could have had that family support earlier, instead of making bad decisions and getting into crazy relationships. I was sneaking into dive clubs when I was seventeen. They were not even checking my ID because I looked a little bit older. I had no business being in there. But nevertheless, I was a teenager going into all these gay clubs where I found women of color who were gay, lesbian, or transgender. But everybody was older than me. I got into the ballroom scene in those clubs, and that's when I was like, *Oh, there are teenagers, and this is a safe place for us to be ourselves.*

I remember a time when you couldn't hold hands in New York. You would get fucked up. They would beat you up; you would get raped if you were a woman; you'd get killed if you were transgender. And that still happens today. But back then it was much more prevalent. You were seeing transgender dead bodies in the Hudson River. Insane. That's the era I grew up in. It was a different time.

And then also I used to spend my summers here in the country. And here, even though I knew some people were gay around town, they're still not talking about it either. So I never came out to my family here. I had a baby, and they just went with that. Then later, in my thirties, I came here with my girlfriend for the family reunion, and that's when they were like, *Oh, okay.* But I never ever told any of my cousins or aunts and uncles here in Frostburg or Cumberland, *I'm gay.* So I technically didn't come out. I mean, they figured it out, but I never verbalized it.

RAE: I'm curious . . . because it sounds like your mom and your family—they weren't stressed about it when you came out, for the most part?

KIJANA: Some of them were stressed out about it. And I know it was because I had already had a child. Back then, it was like, *We don't know if you can raise your child and be gay.* That was a thing, you know?

RAE: Can you talk more about that?

KIJANA: It was a horrible thing to be told that because of my sexual identity, I may not be a good mother, or that I may be influencing my child. That was hard to hear. And it was difficult for me as a young mother to try and deal with that. Back in the day, that was a thing.

It was actually in the court system, too. You know what I mean? If I was born in 1950, I would have been in a psych ward, getting electric shock treatment for being myself, for falling in love and loving women. Like, I can't even. And that wasn't too long ago. But it was very difficult to hear that and to deal with that or to have the person that you had these children with say that they're going to take you to court because you're an unfit mother, because you're lesbian. And, *I don't want that around my child.* I got that. Definitely, definitely, definitely. And it actually put a strain on the relationship that I have with one of my children. I have two children, actually. My daughter is turning thirty-one in August, and my son turned twenty-nine. So, with my youngest son it was always an issue. Because that's what his father spewed. So I have had to deal with that, in my relationship with my own child, that kind of bigotry. And that's something that is still a sore issue. It does affect me, and it has definitely affected our relationships.

RAE: I can only imagine. It sounds awful.

I want to ask you about your family history here. You were saying the other day that your family goes back a long time here.

KIJANA: It does. The Harper family has

been here in Frostburg for over a hundred years. We were part of the original African American families who migrated here. Our family migrated from Oakland, Maryland, to Frostburg during the times when it wasn't favorable to be an African American. Garrett County was a sundown town. So we're one of the oldest African American families here. Frostburg State University [FSU] was actually built on part of my family's land. We're working on getting a plaque put up, because land that the college is on was family land. It's called Brownsville. FSU is actually built on African American land.

RAE: So, your family moved here from another part of Maryland at the time?

KIJANA: We didn't move. We were chased out of Oakland, Maryland, because of racism. I don't know if it was better here in Allegany County, but I know that my great, great-grandmother had a big brood of children. And she bought them all lands. She was very influential in Oakland. She received her inheritance, and she bought land here in Frostburg, and she gave each of her kids land. So that's how most of my family owned land at one point. But a lot of that land has now been bought up.

We've been here for a while. My great-grandmother, Helen Harper, didn't have a farm, but she had a big-ass vegetable garden with every single vegetable and herb that you could think of, and we had a black walnut tree, and she made her own root beer. That was good. And my Uncle Pete, I remember him playing the banjo and the guitar. He's a very well-known musician here in Allegany County. He also had a restaurant on that land where the college is now, and a lot of famous jazz musicians came through there. The Hen House Restaurant, their chicken recipe— that's my Uncle Pete's recipe. Like, the roots here are deep.

That's part of the reason why we have the Brownsville project and why the NAACP [National Association for the Advancement of Colored People] is working to get those reparations, especially to the families that we can document have lived right here for over a hundred years. A part of FSU is built on my family's land. Period. The end. I worked there at the university managing the Lane Dining Hall. One of the dorms is my uncle's house, where I used to play and listen to him play his instruments and cook. We had family dinners at his house. Now it's a dorm. There isn't a plaque that has his name on it. You know what I'm saying? The college acknowledges Brownsville, and the

Brownsville descendants. So, great, you have acknowledged it, but you could do better than that.

But yeah, my family has been here for a long time. I always looked forward to coming up here. My mother kicked me out for three months, bam, *You're going to Frostburg.* And I'd be like, *Yeah!* Because in New York, my mother didn't let me play that much. But here, I could run, I could jump, I could climb trees. I loved coming out here. It wasn't a hard sell for me to move back here. And that's why, when my family asks, "Why are you back here?" I say, "Because I know this area. I grew up here. I'm about the Tastee-Freeze, too, and blue crabs." You know what I'm saying? I remember buying the penny candy right up the road. I have a lot of great memories here. And now, I'm having, and will continue to have, great memories as an adult because of the connection with my family, and because of the connection with my queer community. I'm looking forward to doing more work here. I'm all about this life.

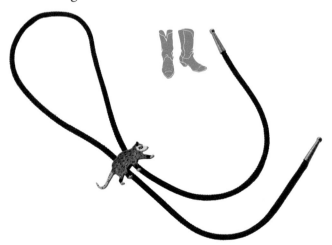

One of the many things I loved about this interview is the way it pushed me to acknowledge some of my assumptions around how much easier all of this is for city queers. Clearly, I know that nothing is that cut and dried and that, especially when looking across different historical periods and other layers of identity including race, LGBTQIA2S+ experiences, even within the same geographic location, vary widely. But it was fascinating to hear Kijana talk about growing up in the middle of New York City, with a mom who was working actively to support the gay community in the midst of the AIDS crisis and still not feeling like she had community, support, or an outlet as a young queer teenager. I also love how directly and concretely Kijana talks about the need for reparations in describing how her family's land is now owned by Frostburg State University, where she worked at the time of this interview. Kijana has since left that job, and in fall 2022 she founded Safe Space Cumberland, a community center, with the intention of unifying and strengthening the local queer community while bringing awareness and visibility to the general public. Safe Space has hosted drag story hours, a speaker series, book clubs, art workshops for youth, and more. You can find them online and support their work at https://www.safespacecumberland.com.

Claire Raven Bishop performing. Photo courtesy of Ty Walker

TY WALKER (he/him), 32 years old

Šaawanwaki (Shawnee) and Massawomeck lands
Cumberland, Maryland
December 16, 2022

During the week I spent in Cumberland in June 2022, I had interviewed Ty Walker's partner, Mary Jane, both formally and backstage at multiple drag shows. I recorded a few moments of audio with Ty in drag as Claire Raven Bishop, just before his first-ever drag performance. Ty was nervous, and told me so, and then slayed and took home a trophy. The ball was emceed by Kijana West, whose excerpt precedes this one. The ballroom event was probably the first to take place in the mountains of western Maryland, and it was one of the most joyful and beautiful parts of that entire week of Pride events. I don't know if Ty would have agreed to an interview with me during that first trip up in June, because he is very shy and mostly stood in the background of events where Mary Jane performed, helping her get ready and taking photos. But after six months of keeping in touch sporadically with Ty and all the other queens, I made the trip back up in December for a holiday drag show. Ty wasn't performing that night—he'd had a rough performance a month before where his wig came off mid-set and he didn't feel ready to go on stage again—so we stood together against the wall throughout the show, Ty in his suit with his camera, me in a sequined blazer trying not to spill my beer on my recorder. I asked Ty if he'd be up for a formal interview with me the next day, and he agreed. I sat down with him at his kitchen table.

RAE: I'm gonna ask you about Cumberland because it's different from Baltimore, where you grew up, right? What are the things you love about Cumberland? And are there things you wish were different about Cumberland?

TY: I like the fact that when I come outside, I can see mountains, and I can see the clouds over the mountains. I can see the sun peeking over the mountains. It wasn't like that in the city. All you saw there was tall buildings and broken neighborhoods. That's it. But the thing I hate about Cumberland . . . it's minor. It's minor because it happens everywhere. I hate that when I go into stores, I'm always getting dirty looks. There are some people who do accept me, but there are some who don't. If I could change the racist looks, I would, but that's something I can't change. I wish I could, but I can't.

The thing I love most is the mountains. I like the small snow globe that we live in, and the fact that I can be free and do drag here. I do like it here. I do. I didn't think I would, to be honest. Because we got here and it was all these mountains and shit, and everybody driving these big-ass trucks. But I got used to it. I mean, you can't get rid of the drug problem. I wish that was gone, but, you know, it happens.

RAE: When we were here in June, am I right that the ball was your first time performing?

TY: Yeah, it was my first time performing anything in life. That was definitely my first time doing anything, winning anything.

When I first heard about it, I ain't gonna lie, I was nervous and all that. I wanted to be there, but I didn't want to be in it. Because I'm like, *Oh my God, I don't know any of this.* I'm afraid, you know, I'm trading out my suit and tie for a different attire. But then the confidence came in because I watched *Legendary*. I got used to watching a whole lot of *RuPaul*[*'s Drag Race*]. You know, and I've recently just watched [*The Boulet Brothers'*] *Dragula*. Watching this *Legendary* ballroom competition . . . I don't know, something made me want to do it. I come from a dancing family, on my mother's side. I mean, everybody dance, act, and sing. I don't usually because I'm a natural-born introvert. But I just had to try it.

When I went out onto the stage, when they called my name for the first time,

especially when I was walking with the house that I was with, I didn't know what type of looks I would get. I ain't gonna lie. Because people know me from being quiet, wearing suits, taking pictures. And it kind of made me scared because I didn't want to be bashed or anything. Because, you know, you give off this demeanor that you're a hardcore guy. You got this wall. And for them to see me like that . . . I didn't want them to think that I was weak or I had a psychotic break or anything. I felt like it was something I had to do. I already dressed in costumes when I used to go to comic conventions, and that was a safe space for me to be in because I was around people who all share the same common interests.

RAE: Wait, did you think that people in the queer community would think you were weak? Or people out in the world? Or both?

TY: Both. Because within the LGB—people know me and Mary Jane; they know us as being a certain way.

RAE: How would you describe it, the way they know you?

TY: They know me as being quiet. I've been told I give off a very intimidating demeanor.

I honestly don't smile in none of my pictures out of drag. They say I have this constant RBF [resting bitch] face. And you know, I don't do it intentionally, it's just how I am. For example, if me and Mary Jane walked into a store—I just stood in the corner, hands behind my back, scoping and observing everything as she went around the store and grabbed all the items she needed. Anyplace where she had to go, I just stood and carried bags.

And in her case, she's, like, the bright and glamorous sunshine that hits people, Mary Jane is. She's a sunshine that hits people. Even my ass. She's the sun, I'm a black hole. That's pretty much how it is, you know? And they say that no light can escape a black hole. I don't know; I don't think no light can enter in it. But Mary Jane was that light that entered in. I mean, as corny as it may sound.

RAE: No, I love that description.

TY: Mary Jane was that light that pierced through that black hole. Now, don't get me wrong, that's only a little speck of light compared to the gravitational pull and being spaghettified and shit. But you get what I mean?

But yeah, I was afraid to go out in drag because I didn't want people to take advantage of me. It's fear. Because I've read stories where people who are drag queens and transgender women—they had some unfortunate events. And, as tough as I am, I was afraid that I would be added to that number. God forbid. Knock on wood.

But I don't know, I kicked it off to the side because, if my partner is doing it, I want to support her, and do it too. So yeah, when I was on that stage floor, in front of the judges and everything, I knew what I had to do. And I told myself, *Yes, I got no experience. I am scared. But one thing I can promise is that I will give people their money's worth.*

RAE: You were amazing! And you won a trophy your first time performing!

TY: Thank you.

RAE: When are you happiest in your life? Just in your day to day, what brings you the most joy?

TY: Oh, it's this place called Coney Island. I don't know if you heard of it? It's a hot dog place. Gino's. Gino makes the best burgers in town. He does. None of his food has ever made it home, 'cause it's that good! Yes, that's my happiest moment, eating one of Gino's burgers from Coney Island. Shit, man, I tell you . . . I'll go down there right now! Like, come on! You had to ask me that question? Oh my goodness. Anything you want on a burger! The ground beef is fresh; it's excellent. You got your cheese on it. I don't even know. He put this secret sauce, or whatever the hell he put on top. It is fucking delicious.

My other happy moment is watching Mary Jane come home from work. And I'm not just saying it. I love watching her come home. She comes home to me and the kids, and they wag they tails, get excited and all that. Of course, I won't admit that to Mary Jane because I'm a hard-ass myself. But I love it when she comes home, because that way I know she's safe and I know that I ain't gonna let nothing happen to her. You know? I love her. And it's different because when I was with a woman, my ex-girlfriend, it was a good relationship. At the time, I did love her

to death and all. But it's different when you're in a relationship with a same-sex person. I don't know why, but I feel like more of a husband to him than I ever was with my ex, and that's a good feeling for me to have. Now I feel like a man who loves his family, and that comes from Mary Jane. The way I feel about him as a male is something I've never felt with a woman, given that I am bisexual. And it's interesting. As you can see, I hold a very high place for her in my mind and my heart. Like I said, she's my gray area, and I want that gray area to stay. I don't want it to be replaced by nothing.

RAE: What do you mean, she's a gray area?

TY: She brings joy in life, and she shows me that not everything is black and white. Not

Ty Walker (left) and Mary Jane (right) in their living room, Cumberland, Maryland, June 2022

everything is just darkness and destruction. I mean, I'm more anarchist than patriot. So my mindset and level of thinking is nothing compared to hers. She is that ray of sunshine. Don't get me wrong: he a fucking hard-ass. I'm sorry, I'm flipping between "he" and "she," you know . . . let's just call her the wife. The wife. Like, it can be hard. Sometimes he does get smart and snaps at me and all that. But ultimately, we do love and care about each other. Sometimes I do wish he would sit down and listen, listen to how much I love him and care about him. And sometimes I feel like it goes in one ear and out the other. And, you know, most of the time, I don't talk about my feelings. Most men like me don't. And that's because of our fathers and how they brought us up, because of how they were raised. But I tried to break that cycle, by showing it more.

But I like a little more gray area. I do.

Like so many shy people, Ty is super funny once you get him talking! As an introvert myself, it always feels like a huge win when I interview a quiet person who opens up and shares all sorts of memories, wisdom, and

wonder with me. Ty shared about growing up rough in Baltimore, his older brother lost to gun violence, his rage at the world after the police murdered Freddie Gray, and his grief about the incarceration of another brother. More than once he said, "I've never told anyone this before," which is always a complicated thing to hear as an oral historian. Ideally, we do create spaces in our interviews that are safe and trusting enough for narrators to talk about anything they want to, and, at the same time, I feel protective of narrators about what they share on recordings—not because we would ever share anything publicly without ongoing rolling consent but because I have so much distrust of the exploitative and voyeuristic ways mainstream media sometimes uses queer and trans stories.

For this excerpt, I decided to give center stage to Ty's love for Mary Jane and his experiences performing in drag for the first time, in part because centering Black joy is fundamental to a project aimed at unsettling narrative tropes about marginalized communities that frequently converge on histories of trauma and violence.

After the interview, I drove away into the dusk of a snowy mountain landscape with no music on, letting the force of his words sink in, as well as deep gratitude that he trusted me enough to share his stories.

Kasha Snyder-McDonald outside the West Virginia Black Pride Foundation, Charleston, West Virginia, July 2023

KASHA SNYDER-MCDONALD she/her, 40-ish years old

Šaawanwaki (Shawnee), S'atsoyaha (Yuchi), and Adena lands
Charleston, West Virginia
July 14, 2023

I first saw Kasha in March 2023 at a rally at the West Virginia state capitol in opposition to the anti-trans bill HB 2007. I didn't get the chance to talk with Kasha there, but I noticed her warm smile and homemade sign and asked if I could make a picture of her. I immediately recognized her onstage at Charleston Pride that June, where I was struck by the way she held that entire crowd in the palm of her hand. I was curious to learn more about her, so I finally reached out on Instagram in early July 2023 and asked if she'd be up for an interview. I met her at a small house on the east side of Charleston, headquarters to the new organization she founded and directs, the West Virginia Black Pride Foundation. We sat inside on a couch with a small window-mounted air-conditioner cranking against the summer heat, between brightly painted walls holding images of Black trans leaders past and present all around us. Kasha is warm and caring, and she checked in multiple times to make sure I was comfortable and to offer me water. She is also fiercely committed to supporting her community, and funny as hell.

KASHA: I always tell people my name is Kasha Snyder-McDonald. I am forty-ish. I am from Charleston, West Virginia, and I am the executive director of West Virginia Black Pride Foundation. The founder, the CEO, the head honcho, that HBIC. All of the above, I'll answer to!

RAE: So you were born and raised in Ashland, it sounds like?

KASHA: Born and raised in Ashland, Kentucky!

RAE: What was your childhood there like? How would you describe Ashland?

KASHA: Golly! Honestly, Ashland was amazing! I was very well liked. I was always the good one, always smiling, always happy. You know, they always had an inkling that I might be gay, and people would call me that as a child, call me "sweet" and stuff. But I was also tough. So if I fought, then they would never ever think that I was gay. So I always had to keep that kind of tough persona, but still fun loving and having a good time and always doing whatever the hell I wanted to. My mom has six kids. Out of the six kids, I was the second born. So I was pretty much left to my own devices. When I was able to start being on my own, like eleven or twelve, I would start finding things to get into myself. There was an old man and an old lady, interracial couple, who lived down the street from me named Audrey and Paul. I would go down there, and Paul would have me sit on the porch, and he would tell me stories. They were like grandparents of mine, and then when Paul died, I would go over and see Audrey. I would do that up until I was, like, golly, sixteen years old. Then she passed away too.

But everything was lovely. I never really thought I had a bad childhood, until graduation time. That's when—I always knew I was gay—but I thought to myself, *You know what, I'm never gonna see these people again. I'm gonna be who I am once I get out of here.* And it did not work out the way that I wanted it to. Because people called me gay at senior breakfast, and I ran out, and I was going to end up fighting two people. My best friend, she was going to fight somebody. And then my other two friends, they was going to fight with me. So we all just left senior breakfast, and people kind of knew, but they didn't know for sure.

Then I left Ashland, and I moved to Florida. Lived in Florida for a couple of years. And when I went to Florida is when I came out. Well . . . rewind. I dated a lot when I

was growing up, to cover up my secret, and I ended up having a son. His name is Z. And I got married because, especially in the Black community, you can't be having no kids and not be married! Also, my mom is Pentecostal. So I was just like, *Oh my gosh!* Plus, I had a kid, I had a house, I had two cars, and everybody was looking up to me because I was the good one in the family. Everybody always thought I was just doing great. And then . . . I just couldn't take it in my soul anymore. There was so much that I just couldn't take, because even though I love my son unconditionally, I didn't want him to see me go through all the things that were getting ready to happen. And I knew that his mom had the resources through her family to take care of him, because her family was okay and well-to-do, and I didn't have that in my family. I didn't want my son growing up thinking that both of his parents hated each other. So I left.

RAE: About how old were you when you left for Florida?

KASHA: I was twentysomething. Twenty-three? It was a few years after Z was born. When I left, I went straight to Florida. I stayed with my best friend, and I came out as gay.

But then, well, I had to come back to Ashland for a while, and I moved in with my big brother. It was around 2008, and my cousin was living here in Charleston. She was like, "Do you want to come to Charleston?" I was like, "I don't know!" Because, like . . . I'm a country girl! And I just didn't really know Charleston like that. I was working at the Outback [Steakhouse] in Ashland, and I was like, "Well, you know what, I'll just transfer my job to Charleston. That way, I'll have a job when I get up there." So I transferred my job. But when I came to look at the Outback here in Charleston, my first impression was *no*, because I've never been around this many Black people before except for my family! And when I got here, it was, like, a lot of Black people, and they was all standing out back of Outback, taking a little break and stuff. And I was like, *Oh, hell no! I'm not* . . . But that was because I was uncomfortable being who I was, and I was too busy worrying about what these people that I never even met was going to be thinking about me.

So, I came to Charleston, and I stayed here. And I was like, *Yeah, okay, I can do this.* I went to Tracks nightclub for the first time. And that was the first time I ever realized that gay people and Black people hung out together. And it was like, *Are you freaking kidding me?!* It was like, *Okay, this is weird. Because there's all these gay people, but then there's all these thugs*—okay, what we consider thugs in the community. And I was like, *Okay, this is crazy!* So I was all excited about it. And I was like, *Okay, well, this is different.* Then I see my drag mother. And she came out, and I was like, "There's no way that's a boy." And they were like, "That is a boy." I was like, "No. It's not." Then she said, "Yes, I am." And then she saw me dance, and she's like, "And you're gonna be my drag daughter!"

RAE: When you said that Tracks was the first place that you saw Black people and gay people hanging out, does that mean that before that you had mostly been like, *Okay, the gay world is white*?

KASHA: Oh, definitely! Yeah. Because in the Black community, we don't talk about gay, at all. And all the bars that I went to in Huntington with my cousin when I was growing up . . . we had went to the Driftwood, and I seen, like, two Black people there. We went to The Stonewall, and there might have been three gay Black people there. And we were them! You know? So it was just, like, a majority of white people. You know, West Virginia.

RAE: Totally. Okay, so then, back to Tracks and the first time you saw your drag mother. You were like—

KASHA: "No, she is not a guy." And they was like, "No, she is a guy." Then she came and introduced herself to me as Alexa. I was out there on the dance floor, dancing. And she's like, "Oh, who is this bitch out here dancing?" I knew how to grab people's attention; that's one thing I did know. So I was like, *I'm gonna dance out here because I know they gonna think I'm the shit.* But then, she can dance too! So I was like, *Oh, shit, she can really dance!* So then she was like, "Well, you're gonna be my daughter." Because I guess she had never seen anybody like me before, and I'd never seen anybody like her either.

RAE: So, you'd seen drag before, but it was just something about her?

KASHA: I'd seen drag before, but it was all white.

RAE: Ah, I see.

KASHA: And when I'd seen drag before, it scared me, 'cause . . . I don't like clowns. [*Laughter*]. I'm just saying! I don't like clowns! [*Laughter*]

RAE: Oh my god, that really made me laugh! So it sounds like you kind of both saw each other and were like—well, she was definitely like, *You're coming with me*? What did you think?

KASHA: I was like, *Okay!* Because I needed a friend, and that was the first time I found gay Black people. Then, when I found gay Black people, I was just like, *Oh my gosh! There's gay Black people!* And then I stopped working at Outback, and I started working at this Italian restaurant called Grazie that opened up at the Town Center Mall. It was very posh, and that was right up my alley. They already used to call me bougie back home in Kentucky, so I was like, *Uh huh! This is right up my alley! I can do this.* And it made good money. My first day there, I met another Black guy, and his name was Michael, and he was light skinned. And me and Michael just hit it off, right then and there. And then we found a bisexual Black girl. And then we just had a clique of friends, and everybody just loved us.

So I started working at Grazie, and I was living with my cousin. And her mother said to me one day, "You have to move because my other daughter is coming with her boyfriend, and there's not enough room in this house." I was like, *Well, shit, y'all asked me to come up in this bitch!* So, at that moment in time, I was like, *You know what, you don't know me all that well, but I'm a very resilient woman—you know, "bitch" is what I would say—and you ain't gonna hold me because I'm proud.* I'm not a person to run back home and have somebody say "I told you so." She said I had to be out by the end of the week, and I had that whole week to work. So I took all the money that I made, and I had enough to get an apartment. The landlord let me pay the deposit through my rent. So I gave him the money. He gave me the keys. And her mom was kind of nasty about it, 'cause she told me I had to sit outside and wait while she went to work because she was afraid that I was going to go in the house and take stuff to fill up my apartment. I'm just like, *I'm not that kind of person. I lived with you for almost damn near a month, and that's what you think of me?*

So I got the little bit of stuff I came with, and I went to the dollar store, and I had just enough money to buy some pillows. My cousin and her girlfriend brought me some things: a Jambox speaker, some food, and beer. And all my friends came over, and we sat down and had a little kiki and party, and everybody was like, "Oh my god! I can't believe you got your apartment!" But on the inside I was scared as fuck because I was like, *I'm on my own in a city that I have no fucking idea about.* And it was scary.

RAE: And you'd only been here like a month?

KASHA: I'd been here less than a month, about three and a half weeks. So after everybody left, I turned on the Jambox, and I went in my bedroom and closed the door. I locked the front-room door because I was still nervous. Before I knew this area, it scared me, because I'm from Kentucky! I'm used to living in the suburbs, like, *hello*?

RAE: Small town.

KASHA: Yeah, right! So I come here, and I was just like, *What the fuck?* So, I closed the door, drank the beer, and I cried myself to sleep. And I woke up the next morning and I said, *You can do anything.* And I have never stopped. I just keep going, and that is something that is really in my head. It seems like I always keep finding different ways to keep me from going forward. Like, you know, being trans is just another step back. They was okay that I was a gay guy, but they cannot stand that we have a trans woman, and especially one that looks like me. Because not only am I Black, but I'm pretty.

RAE: It's true!

KASHA: And I'm very aware because . . . I was always called ugly. So when I transitioned and I had something to do with that, I made sure that that was not what people wanted to say about me. Even when I did drag for a long time, they was always saying my makeup was too harsh. Stuff like that. My drag parents would say if I didn't win pageants, I should quit. I mean, people were very harsh on me. They used to call me "cigarette ashes and glitter"; they used to call me "Juwanna Man," all these negative things. And they were mean to me, all the time. Even when I won Miss Pride of West Virginia, I was told I "fell through the cracks." People didn't clap for me.

And it took *years*, even after I won the biggest pageant in the state of West Virginia, for people to actually even notice me. In the last couple of years, they've really started noticing me because I've started a nonprofit organization, so now they *really* see me. But that's because I don't care anymore. You're *going* to see me. I love my chocolate skin. For such a long period of my life, people made me feel like me being Black was the worst thing I can be, made me feel like being dark Black is the worst thing I can be. And I got sick and tired of it. I don't give a fuck. I love

me now, and I'm so mad at myself for not loving me sooner. That's what sucks. Because if I knew me then, I would probably be farther than I am.

But it's okay because I'm on the right track. I know which direction I'm going. I know what I want to do. Our next big project is amazing, and I can't *wait*! We're going to have a retreat wellness center, and it's going to be the first of its kind here in the state of West Virginia, because that's what West Virginia Black Pride does. We are the first of the first of the first. We do the things that other people talk about. You're going to talk about it? Well, we're going to do it. Yeah, we're gonna make a space!

All these people talk about it. You know what? I'll make a space for us here, y'all. I ain't got no money! I'm an entertainer. I spend all my money on running this foundation. I don't have a job. My job is working at the bar. I'm just now starting to get these speaking engagements too, because I didn't know that that was a thing. But now that I am in the position that I am—the first Black trans woman to run a nonprofit in the state, the first Black LGBTQ+ center run by a Black trans woman as well—so now, a lot of people are reaching out.

Sometimes it can be kind of confusing because you don't know if they're reaching out to be good for you or if they're reaching out to be bad. Because sometimes people want to use us because we fit all the quotas. We're Black owned. We're LGBTQ+. We're trans owned. You know? So we fit all DEI [diversity, equity, and inclusion] quotas for everybody. And instead of people helping us get these grants, they want to get them themselves, and then give us a little bit of money. So they want to use us, and they don't want to help anybody.

But all I want to do—really, *all I want to do*—is get this retreat wellness center.

It's going to be a place where you can come, you can go camping, and just relax, and get away, and breathe, and find solace. And just be in touch with nature. Put your feet in the grass, touch a tree. You know what I'm saying? Because we come from the ground. We come from the waters, we come from all of this, and it's healing. You know when you're in a swimming pool and how relaxing that is? It's because you are of water. You know when you're walking on the ground and you feel calm? It's because you are of dirt. And it's healing. I know what that feels like, and I want everybody else to be able to feel this. I want them to wake up with the sun beaming down on their face. Or, if it's rainy, to get to be in your little cabin, with the rain falling down and the windows open. Or, if it's snowing, to be in your cabin watching the lake freeze over. I want these things. Yeah. We're gonna have it soon.

I often leave interviews feeling like we've only just scratched the surface. We'd spent two hours talking, and I felt like I easily could have interviewed Kasha for twice as many more. There is so much that I appreciate in this interview: I love the way that Kasha describes Charleston (population ~48,000) as feeling like a big city after growing up in Ashland. I love Kasha's account of finding Black queer community for the first time in West Virginia—a story that in and of itself contradicts almost every national media depiction of the state I've ever seen. I love how clearly Kasha's unwavering commitment to supporting her community, no matter what it takes, shines through. I also deeply appreciate her naming the ways in which other organizations use proximity to the West Virginia Black Pride Foundation to fundraise for themselves but don't actually support the work in tangible ways. That tokenization of Black and Brown trans leaders, which is all too common, is also

something I think about often in this project. How do we structure community oral history projects to prioritize the documentation of a diverse range of experiences and identities without replicating patterns of tokenization? Also, 2023 is the first time that I have seen significant trans-led organizing in the state of West Virginia, and it is so exciting to see this leadership emerging here.

After our interview, I made a brief post on the Country Queers Instagram sharing this photo of Kasha and a brief description of her work, including that she hopes to start a retreat center. A few days later, I received messages from Kasha and her communications volunteer that someone reached out to them after seeing that post and donated the use of a farm an hour north of Charleston for WVBP. At the time of writing, they have hosted a few volunteer work parties on the land, but there is much more work ahead. Please head over to their website and make a generous donation to this important work: https://wvbpfoundation.com.

POSTSCRIPT

"A WHOLENESS TO OUR LIVES"

A CONVERSATION BETWEEN HERMELINDA CORTÉS AND RAE GARRINGER

I've long been a fan of hermelinda cortés's sharp analysis and dedication to rural people. In fall 2023, the two of us had a conversation reflecting on the project, its work in the world, and its future. In the spirit of deep collaboration that marks the Country Queers ethos, we close with an excerpt from that conversation. You can find a full transcript on the Country Queers website.

HERMELINDA: I'm interested in hearing how it feels to think of yourself as a pin between generations of LGBTQ people who happen to reside in rural and country spaces. Our generation—we are bridges between the Suzanne [Pharr]s and the Dorothy [Allison]s of the world and the young people in county high schools who are hosting walkouts in defense of LGBTQ people and against the horrible policies that are rolling out at school boards across the country right now. . . . Through this work, we do become critical knowledge keepers, if nothing else.

RAE: Honestly, the hardest part for me has been having to become a slightly public figure. It is really uncomfortable for me to be the host, to be interviewed, to have to leave this mountainside with animals all around. I'm deeply uncomfortable with the attention. And it does feel like a lot of pressure—for me to think and articulate complex things quickly—that just isn't my pace of being. So it's hard for me to see myself as a pin between generations or in the lineage of Suzanne and Dorothy, who I admire so much.

I don't always know exactly what the project has done in the world, because it's hard for me to get enough distance from it to see that. But, when Country Queers started, you could not find rural queer stories online. And there's so much more visibility of our experiences now, which is great! But there's a new frustration I have, where it feels like this new visibility is somehow still missing the point. People know that country queers exist now. Great. Finally. Thanks. We've accomplished that, at least, right? But is that all we get? And I don't know if it's Orville Peck's tour or what, but this summer *all* the queers on the internet have their cowboy outfits—like, what the fuck just happened? You know what I mean? It feels like everybody's got a Western shirt. Everybody's got cowboy boots and a bolo tie. In LA, in New York, in the Bay. Everybody's got a cowboy outfit. Which is cool! I'm into cowboys! I love the aesthetic. But *that's* not the end goal.

HERMELINDA: No, and it's this commodification of the identity.

RAE: Totally. And there's much more visibility, but is there actually any more interest from folks in cities around listening to our stories, around respecting our experiences and expertise, and building solidarity with us? I'm not sure there is.

Just in this past year, there have been political and physical attacks—at bars, the substation shooting in North Carolina,[*] the [November 2022 Club Q] shooting in Colorado Springs, Proud Boys showing up to queer events across the country. And rural and small-town areas are in a different place in terms of the intensity and escalation of violence than we were when this project started. I worry about the rural queer and trans folks in places like Utah, or parts of rural West Virginia, where they're completely outnumbered by Proud Boys and militias.

---

[*] In December 2022, two electrical substations in Moore County, North Carolina, were shot up, knocking out power for over forty thousand people in central North Carolina during a winter cold snap. The shootings took place during a drag show in a nearby small town called Southern Pines. Event organizers had faced online threats and harassment in the weeks before to the show, leading many local LGBTQIA2S+ people to wonder if the substation attack was connected. For more on these attacks, see Hannah Schoenbaum, "North Carolina Power Grid Attack Stokes Fear in Rural LGBTQ Community," NBC News, December 9, 2022, https://www.nbcnews.com/nbc-out/out-news/north-carolina-power-grid-attack-stokes-fear-rural-lgbtq-community-rcna60945.

HERMELINDA: And in a lot of our counties, that's just how it is, right? That is part of what the project is going to have to navigate. Because that is a real concern for many of us. It was most poignant to me in the interview with the old dykes out with their guns [Mason Michael]. In reading that, I was like, *Oh, we're ramping back up to that moment.* That's part of the reason I point to—not just me and you but humans who sit in particular seats, with particular skills, in a particular moment of time. That to me is part of the question of the future of Country Queers. It's not just for the project; it is a question for us as individuals and for the larger moment beyond us. And it's why some of the future of Country Queers is not in our control. It will evolve into what the conditions both allow for and require of it.

This is one of your strengths—to allow that to unfold. I see you as a doula of the project. And what it means to be a doula is different from what it means to be the person who is giving birth and is different from what it means to be the primary caregiver after birth. That's what I mean by asking about the future of the project.

RAE: When I think about all the details behind the scenes of the project, and trying to figure out how it will work, who will run it, and how to fund it, I get totally overwhelmed about the future. But I don't think the work of Country Queers is over.

Continuing to document our histories still feels important to me because they already have been almost entirely erased. And part of what this rising wave of legislation and violence is aimed at doing is erasing our ability to know that we have always been here, that we are still here.

HERMELINDA: And all each of us can do is to keep our stories and our lives from getting erased, and in communicating that, there is a wholeness to our lives. That is one of the things that the project has done beautifully and will continue to do.

Country Queers has also given people a vehicle to see part of their own experience reflected. And that is what the best storytelling does: it allows us to see a part of ourselves. That, to me, is the most powerful narrative change work.

There's a very particular thing that oral stories do for a community. I was at SONG Gaycation the summer that [the 2016] Pulse [nightclub] shooting happened. It was the last morning, and everybody was about to leave. I was up early with the sun, getting all these notifications, and I started writing a press release on my phone because I was the communications director. The night before, I'd interviewed a bunch of SONG elders around the fire about their experiences in the eighties and nineties. At least two of them talked about being at gay bars when they had gotten bombed. The next morning was a really profound moment for me. The people who had heard those stories the night before, who then heard what had happened at Pulse—it was easier for them to survive the moment because they had this other set of stories to hold on to, to know that other people had survived too.

That is also what Country Queers has done. It has given our people the balm of stories of others who have survived and thrived.

ACKNOWLEDGMENTS

project of this scale and scope is never only one person's work. There are more people to name than space or my memory will allow, but I want to include here a sincere thank you to everyone who has made this project possible. It was incredibly difficult to narrow this manuscript down to the handful of narrator excerpts that appear here. To each person who has shared your story with this project, thank you. *Country Queers* wouldn't exist without you, and the generosity with which you opened your homes and lives is a gift I'll never forget. *Country Queers* also wouldn't exist without: our volunteer transcriptionists, everyone who has donated, conversations with friends at Appalshop, Highlander, Project South, SONG, the STAY Project, the National Council of Elders, and Out in the Open, the grants and awards we've received, and the support and patience of friends and family who have listened to me worry about it all, for *years*.

This book has been a wild bronc to wrangle, and I could write a whole chapter of gratitude for the folks who kept me going through the process. In no particular order, and with apologies to any I've missed, thank you to Sarah Wadsworth, Ada Smith, Yasmine Chakar Farhang, Sam Hamlin, Kendall Bilbrey, Willa Johnson, Lani Blechman, Sara Balnionis, Sage Blymyer, Ariana Deignan Kosmides, Sarryn Shapero, Ash-Lee Woodard Henderson, Jai Arun Ravine and George Beckner, Stephanie Tyree, Blair Campbell, Elizabeth Falcon, Sophie Ziegler, HB Lozito, Liz Sanders, Annie Jane Cotton, Annie Terrafranca, Deya Terrafranca, Nia Lee, and Mistress Blunt. Endless gratitude for my ROMP crew: Diikahnéhi Delaronde, Lauren Garretson, Steph Guilloud, Brandon Sun Eagle Jent, Pumpkin Starr, and Joe Tolbert. Steph G. gets an extra shout-out for being an excellent first reader of segments of this book, as does Diikahnéhi for the generous feedback, review of, and advice on best approaches to naming Indigenous peoples. Thanks to my LA writing crew: Taz Ahmed, Allison De La Cruz, D'lo, Erin O'Brien, and Anu Yadav; to my parents: Lynn, Jeff, and Dan, my siblings: Cail, Kristen, and David, and my niece: Reyah; to my Terrafranca-Wadsworth family; to Lynn Benedict, the greatest goat mentor of all time; and to my brilliant therapist!

Thank you to manuscript readers Nathalie Nia Faulk, Adrienne Keene, hermelinda cortés, Fanny Julissa García, and Maria Isabelle Carlos for the attention, care, and smarts each of you brought to the draft. Thank you to Suzanne Pharr for all the lessons, for our friendship, and for the book's foreword. Thank you to the podcast editorial advisory dream team, who are so much more than that: hermelinda cortés, Sharon P. Holland, and Lewis Raven Wallace. There are no words to describe how humbled and grateful I remain that you said yes to the invitation in 2020 and for all your continued support since. Thank you, Lou Murrey, for the author photos and visit!

Thanks to the Voice of Witness Storyteller Initiative and editorial team, the Southern Movement Media Fund of Press On, and the West Virginia Humanities Council Fellowship for early and crucial support in the writing of this book. Thank you to the *entire* Haymarket team for taking a risk on this little homegrown project and making my book dream come true! Special thanks to Eric Kerl for shepherding the visual design. Endless gratitude to Dao X. Tran for showing up in my inbox in June 2022, at a time when I felt like giving up on this work entirely. Every scrappy, rural, DIY oral history project needs a fairy godmother, and you are ours.

Finally, thank you to my animal family, for so much joy and the reminder that humans are the weakest link, and to these West Virginia mountains, for teaching me the power of stillness and commitment.

Photo by Lou Murrey. loumurrey.com

RAE GARRINGER (they/them) is a writer, oral historian, and audio producer who grew up on a sheep farm in southeastern West Virginia, and now lives a few counties away on S'atsoyaha (Yuchi) and Šaawanwaki (Shawnee) lands. They are the founder of Country Queers, a multimedia oral history project documenting rural and small town LGBTQIA2S+ experiences since 2013. When not working with stories, Rae spends a lot of time failing at keeping goats in fences, swimming in the river, and two-stepping around their trailer.

ABOUT HAYMARKET BOOKS

HAYMARKET BOOKS is a radical, independent, nonprofit book publisher based in Chicago. Our mission is to publish books that contribute to struggles for social and economic justice. We strive to make our books a vibrant and organic part of social movements and the education and development of a critical, engaged, and internationalist Left.

We take inspiration and courage from our namesakes, the Haymarket Martyrs, who gave their lives fighting for a better world. Their 1886 struggle for the eight-hour day—which gave us May Day, the international workers' holiday—reminds workers around the world that ordinary people can organize and struggle for their own liberation. These struggles—against oppression, exploitation, environmental devastation, and war—continue today across the globe.

Since our founding in 2001, Haymarket has published more than nine hundred titles.

Radically independent, we seek to drive a wedge into the risk-averse world of corporate book publishing. Our authors include Angela Y. Davis, Arundhati Roy, Keeanga-Yamahtta Taylor, Eve Ewing, Aja Monet, Mariame Kaba, Naomi Klein, Rebecca Solnit, Olúfẹ́mi O. Táíwò, Mohammed El-Kurd, José Olivarez, Noam Chomsky, Winona LaDuke, Robyn Maynard, Leanne Betasamosake Simpson, Howard Zinn, Mike Davis, Marc Lamont Hill, Dave Zirin, Astra Taylor, and Amy Goodman, among many other leading writers of our time. We are also the trade publishers of the acclaimed Historical Materialism Book Series.

Haymarket also manages a vibrant community organizing and event space in Chicago, Haymarket House, the popular Haymarket Books Live event series and podcast, and the annual Socialism Conference.